New India in the 21ˢᵗ Century

21 VISIONS FOR A DEVELOPED INDIA BY 2050

Dr. SHISHIR SRIVASTAVA

Author of **The Eight Powers Within You**

ISBN 979-8-89067-673-3

This book is dedicated to the

'Father of New India'

Shri. Narendra Modi ji

Hon'ble Prime Minister of India,

who has given hope and shown light to over a billion Indians, by working day and night to steer India

on the path towards becoming a Developed Nation.

apro/jg/dt/2013/11/02

Date : 02-11-2013

Message

Development requires foresight and vision. Development and growth indicates life and aspirations of being in the mainstream. Children and the Youth of India are the true future of our nation. This future of India, the youth, must be nurtured with knowledge, vision and empowered with will to execute !

I am happy to learn that a book **"New India in the 21st Century: Collection of 21st inspiring visions"** is being published to empower the youth of India. I hope the book will be proved really useful and inspiring for **future Indians.**

(Narendra Modi)

To,
Shree Shishir Srivastava,
248/15, Lakar Mandi,
Nr. Jai Hanuman Temple,
Yahiya Ganj, Lucknow – 226 003
(Uttarpradesh)
Emal : author@shishirsrivastava.org

Narendra Modi
Chief Minister, Gujarat State

आज़ादी का
अमृत महोत्सव

Date: 21.08.2023

Message

I am happy to know that a famous academician, **Dr. Shishir Srivastava** has written a book named **'New India in the 21st Century: 21 Visions for a Developed India by 2050'** showcasing the India's potential, challenges, and future possibilities.

This book presents an outline of the forthcoming progress and advancement of our great nation by 2050. Different viewpoints about India's growth journey amid ongoing global changes and challenges have been underlined in this book. India has achieved significant success in the socio-economic field. After becoming the fifth-largest economy in the world, India is now poised to become the third major economic power. India is destined to become the 'Vishwa Guru' under the dynamic leadership of the visionary Prime Minister Shri Narendra Modi Ji. I hope that this book will be immensely helpful for the readers.

I congratulate Dr. Shishir Srivastava on their forthcoming book and wish for its successful publication.

With good wishes,

(Rajnath Singh)

Office : Room No. 104, Ministry of Defence, South Block, New Delhi-110011
Tel. : +91 11 23012286, +91 11 23019030, Fax : +91 11 23015403
E-mail : rmo@mod.nic.in

Message from Gurudev Sri Sri Ravi Shankar

India has seen many phases and turns of ups and downs throughout history. What has kept India alive, where so many other civilizations flourished and perished, is the stream of spiritual knowledge that has continued to flow unbroken through time. In fact, the ebb and flow of India's growth has always been linked with its spirituality. If we look back, we find that prosperity was at its peak here when spirituality was at its peak. As spirituality diminished, so did India's prosperity.

Unfortunately, spirituality has wrongly been taken to mean leaving everything and going off to the forest, to live in caves. People ask me, "Gurudev, you teach meditation. Why do you get involved in social issues like corruption?" No. Love for God and service to society are not different, they are one. You will find this all across the history of India. True lovers of God have always cared for society. They don't go and run to caves in the Himalayas. Only those who are afraid, who have not attained do that out of fear of deviating from their path. Those who are strong work while remaining in society. The enormous energy you gain from spiritual practices has to be used to uplift society. Once you realize your innate power, you don't need a seat or position to serve people. You can do better without a formal post like Mahatma Gandhi did. Often a ruler is not a reformer and a reformer doesn't rule. That is why in the ancient days, sages used to provide counsel to the kings in case something was being overlooked in the kingdom and steps had to be taken for it.

India is unique in the world just for the sheer amount of diversity available in every sphere here, be it geography, language, culture, dress, food or just the ways of living. Keeping this in mind, there are seven areas in which India stands out and can be proud of but that have not fully been explored yet.

1. **Tourism**: India has such variety of geographical landscape that's not available in any one country in the world. We have hills and mountains, rivers, beaches, plateaus, forests that can be easily developed as international tourist attractions. Being the oldest living civilization in the world, so many sites all over the country carry such a long history related to them that people find so interesting. The carvings and sculptures in our ancient structures tell the story of an extremely rich cultural heritage. Many universities outside have courses on Indian culture but we have not showcased it to the world.

2. **Food**: If you travel around India, after every few miles or kilometers, you will find different varieties of food. Once, I said, just out of curiosity, 'Let's have a vegetarian food festival in India', and our volunteers prepared 5600 food items - seven tons of different type of food. This *Annam Brahmam* program that we had in Ahmedabad had so many dishes that we had never heard of. And this variety was just from Gujarat. If you go to Tripura, which is a small state, even they have hundreds of varieties of food items and preparations which are not known to the general public. Similarly there are many special dishes in South India - *Obbatu, Chutney Pudi, Gojju, Villakai* that North Indians are not aware of and vice versa.

3. **Music and Dance**: Indian classical music and classical dance is such a deep body of knowledge that it takes decades to learn and gain mastery over. The way that various emotions and feelings find expression through our dance and music is exquisite and matchless. We have seen that the West deeply appreciates these art forms from India but they can be highlighted much more.

4. **Dress and Jewelry**: Before medieval times, Indian garments used to be imported to Europe and were in big demand there. The Indian dress is appreciated the world over but we have no pride in our ethnic dress. There are many social clubs where Indian dress like kurta-pyjama is not allowed. Similarly, Indian jewelry has been famous the world over for centuries. India introduced diamonds to the world and still has the largest diamond cutting and polishing industry.

5. **Information Technology**: The whole world recognizes our strength in this field now.

6. **Ayurveda**: Ayurveda is a complete system of medicine that is 5000 years old. It is time-tested and is fast becoming the system of the future. Despite all the technology, modern medicine has not succeeded in providing total health care. People are realizing all over the world that the mind and the body are related and treating just the physical body is not sufficient. Ayurveda has always had a holistic view of health that recognizes not just the harmony between the mind and body in an individual but also between the individual and Nature.

7. **Yoga and meditation**: Spirituality has been India's gift to the world but we have not valued it ourselves. Yoga is a 27 billion dollar industry in just the USA itself and is 99% dominated by local Americans. They have marketed yoga, which is a product of India, much better than us. People are invited to do mantra and chanting in some buildings in New York but all across India, if someone is chanting in temples, we don't even bother to look at them. When I travel across India, I ask in a gathering,

"How many people have read the Bhagvad Gita?" I see only a few hands go up in a crowd of thousands. New York University Press has published Yoga Vasistha for its students but very few people in India itself know that such a scripture exists at all. The depth and knowledge given in Patanjali Yoga Sutras or Ashtavakra Gita or Tripura Rahasya leaves one wonderstruck. The system of education that we follow has made this wealth of knowledge and wisdom unavailable to us.

India has marched forward for centuries with its head held high and will reach higher peaks in the centuries to come. Some people sit like spectators and some people actively participate. If you sit like a spectator, you will fall into inertia. But if you are among those who participate, there is no end to your happiness. We are passing through a phase of intense transformation. Let's steer our lives in such a direction that we can contribute to this transformation. Let's stand as agents of change in the nation. Let's volunteer for a better India.

– Gurudev Sri Sri Ravi Shankar
Humanitarian Leader and Spiritual Teacher
Founder, Art of Living Foundation

Message from Dr. Vikram Singh

I was immensely delighted to go through the manuscript of the treatise entitled '**New India in the 21ˢᵗ Century**: *21 Visions for a Developed India by 2050*' a scholarly book written by Dr. Shishir Srivastava, an academician of great repute, who has vast insight and experience of painstaking research, nationally and Internationally!

This study visualizes the road map and the consequent difficult journey that India has already undertaken under the dynamic leadership of India's visionary Prime Minister, Shri Narendra Modi ji, an icon of patriotism and selfless service. India is indeed destined to become the Vishwa Guru, as predicted by Swami Vivekananda and as elaborately explained by Dr. Shishir Srivastava, who proves this with incontrovertible evidence and statistics that India was plundered by the British of 47 trillion dollars, during the colonial rule. But a mature leadership has made India the fifth largest economy in the world, in the year 2022 at 3.7 trillion dollars, with a growth rate of 7.7% of GDP.

India is poised to go higher still, at 5 trillion dollar economy and become the third major economic power, globally in the near future.

India's demographic dividend, the youth workforce, the quality education incorporating, the best international practices and the futuristic technologies that will galvanize the nation as a major industrial manufacturing hub and consequently transforming India into a major world power. India has skillfully managed the fast evolving Geopolitical changes, balancing the decline of US power, oil and energy compulsions with astute diplomatic and financial compulsions.

I would complement Dr. Shishir for his elaborate studies in Geneva and extensive research of almost 10 years! A study and dedication that is nothing short of 'Tapasya'.

This book would be invaluable for students and researchers of geopolitics, diplomacy and current affairs. In fact, such detailed analysis and study would not have been possible unless one had hands-on experience and international exposure, which the learned author, Dr. Shishir Srivastava can proudly claim!

With all my good wishes and blessings,

– Dr. Vikram Singh IPS (retd.)
Former Director-General of Police, U.P.
Chancellor, Noida International University, Noida

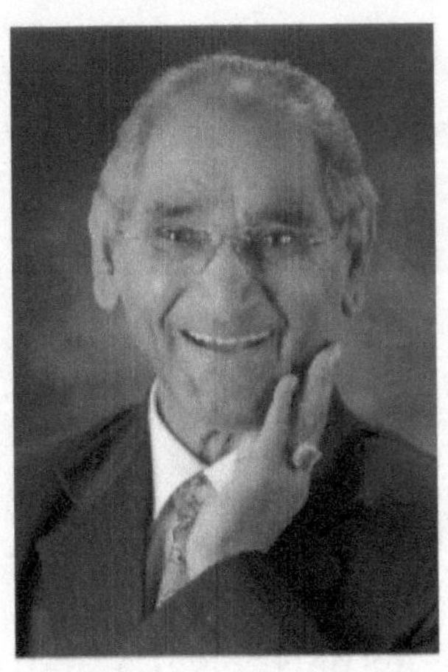

Message from Dr. Jagdish Gandhi

I am delighted that the book '**New India in the 21**st **Century:** *21 Visions for a Developed India by 2050*' by Dr. Shishir Srivastava is a profound exploration of India's path to becoming a developed nation by 2050.

Dr. Srivastava's book underscores India's rich heritage and the potential of its youthful population. He outlines a comprehensive roadmap for India's development across 21 key areas, drawing from the nation's recent achievements and strong leadership. The book explores how India can leverage economic reforms, IT prowess, education, and infrastructure for sustainable growth. Each chapter adopts a three-fold approach, reflecting on past successes, offering practical plans for progress, and painting an optimistic picture of India in 2050 if these plans are diligently pursued. From education to healthcare, gender equality, sustainable development, and more, the book provides pragmatic strategies inspired by developed nations.

Dr. Srivastava's vision extends beyond economic growth, emphasizing inclusive development where every citizen actively contributes. It addresses critical factors like governance, digital transformation, renewable energy, cultural preservation, and global diplomacy, positioning India as a global leader by 2050. "New India in the 21st Century" is a compelling call to action, urging collaboration among citizens, government, and institutions to nurture a positive society and empower India's youth. With its forward-looking approach, the book inspires hope for a prosperous India, contributing significantly to global progress and prosperity.

Readers will gain deep insights into India's potential, the challenges it must overcome, and the opportunities that lie ahead. Dr. Srivastava's insightful exploration vividly portrays a united New India, driven by purpose and determination, confidently advancing toward a brighter future by 2050.

I encourage you to embark on this enlightening journey through the pages of "New India in the 21st Century" and join us in shaping a remarkable tomorrow for our beloved nation.

– Dr. Jagdish Gandhi
Founder Manager
City Montessori School (CMS), Lucknow
(World's largest school with over 61,000 students
and Laureate of UNESCO Prize for Peace Education)

Contents

21 Visions for a Developed India by 2050

Preface

New India in the 21ˢᵗ Century: *21 Visions for a Developed India by 2050* presents ideas and proposals that could have a positive effect on the development of the Nation as a whole. During the last decade, India has exercised strong leadership both domestically and internationally. The visions mentioned in this book could further help steer India towards a 'developed nation' status.

The book represents the aspiration of Indians who wish to see their motherland revive its Ancient Glory. It also gives hope to the Indian diaspora and global citizens worldwide who wish to see India and Indians becoming prosperous and leading the world economically and spiritually. It explores 21 key areas which are important for India's overall development. Each chapter is divided into three sub-parts. The first part traces the recent achievements of India while the second part elaborates on how India can harness its potential in certain areas to become a developed nation through the plan of action. The third part presents what the future of India will look like in 2050 if India continues to follow the plan of action laid out in the second part. In a nutshell, this book presents a road map which explores 'where we are coming from?' and 'what we have to do further on?' as well as 'where we are heading?' and 'how we can get there?'

I conceptualized this book in 2013 and over the last decade, India's position has improved greatly and at present it is recognized globally. I was on a four-month study leave to do a short-term course in International Relations at the Geneva School of Diplomacy and International Relations (GSD) in Switzerland from February to

May 2023. During this period, I studied Global Environment Policies & Sustainability, Geopolitics and International Law. Through this study, I gained exposure to lectures and special seminars conducted by eminent professors in Geneva. My professor in Geopolitics, Dr. Alexander Lambert, encouraged me to do a case study on 'India Evolving as a Geopolitical Pivot' and while I was researching for this case study, I thought of finally penning down this book.

As you go through this book, I hope that you will realize the possibilities that India can explore by harnessing its rich cultural roots combined with the strength of its massive youth population to achieve sustainable development in all spheres. We have many miles to go to attain excellence in the fields of education, scientific innovation and research; improve infrastructure; foster good Governance and also boost manufacturing and industry.

India's progress towards becoming a developed nation is driven by factors such as its demographic dividend, economic reforms, IT and services sector, education and skilled workforce, infrastructure development, manufacturing sector growth, entrepreneurship and start-up culture, social-welfare programs, renewable-energy infrastructure and global engagement.

To achieve equitable and prosperous growth, India needs to address disparities in sectors that lag. This can be accomplished by focusing on inclusive development in areas such as agriculture, rural development, education, healthcare, research and development, transparency in governance, manufacturing growth, gender equality, science and technology, cultural preservation, global diplomacy, ease-of-doing-business, digitalization, defence and security, tourism promotion, sports and fitness and international collaboration.

To make India a developed country, every citizen must take responsibility to contribute the best towards their respective fields. By implementing strategies in the areas I suggest, India could realize its potential, become a developed nation and contribute to global progress and prosperity. I hope that you enjoy reading this book. I invite you to share your valuable feedback with me via email: shishir.india2015@gmail.com

– Dr. Shishir Srivastava

Acknowledgement

I thank you for picking up this book as you aspire to see a developed India and a developed World.

This book is dedicated to all the youth of our country who aspire to see a developed India in the 21st Century.

I would like to thank my wife, Sophia, for all her support throughout our journey together; I am also grateful to my son, Srijan, for placing his confidence in me which helped me write this book.

I remain thankful to CMS founders, Dr. Jagdish Gandhi and Dr. Bharti Gandhi, as well as CMS MD & President, Prof. Geeta Gandhi Kingdon for their inspiration, guidance and support.

– Dr. Shishir Srivastava

India on the Road to Becoming a Developed Country

Defining a Developed Country

A developed country is characterized by high per capita income, a strong and diverse economy, advanced industries and well-developed infrastructure. It prioritizes human development which includes education, healthcare and quality-of-life indicators. Developed countries have low poverty and inequality levels and robust social-welfare systems; they promote social justice and equal opportunities. They have efficient infrastructure and public services, stable political systems, good governance and respect for human rights.

India's achievements during the last decade

India has been focusing on economic growth and the implementation of reforms to sustain the same. Initiatives like 'Make in India', 'Digital India' and 'GST' were aimed at boosting manufacturing, digitalization and streamlining taxation. The government invested in infrastructure development—including transportation networks—through projects like Bharatmala, Sagarmala and the Smart Cities Mission. These efforts were made to enhance connectivity, urban development and maintain overall infrastructure quality.

India recognizes the importance of a skilled workforce and has implemented programs and initiatives to promote skill development and vocational training. Efforts are also underway to improve the quality of education, expand access to education and foster research and innovation. India is making progress in technological advancements through initiatives like 'Digital India', and also promoting digital literacy, e-governance and adoption of digital technologies. The government also focuses on research and development, entrepreneurship and leveraging emerging technologies such as artificial intelligence, blockchain and renewable energy.

India prioritizes sustainable development for long-term prosperity and has implemented measures to promote renewable energy, reduce carbon emissions and address environmental challenges. Initiatives like the 'International Solar Alliance' and 'Swachh Bharat Abhiyan' (Clean India Mission) focus on sustainable practices, clean energy and the improvement of sanitation and hygiene. The government is committed to promoting a greener and cleaner India.

How can India progress further?

India has made great progress, but it needs to address some more challenges to achieve its vision of becoming a developed nation. Poverty alleviation is a key focus, which requires effective social-welfare programs and inclusive economic policies. Strengthening healthcare infrastructure and improving access to quality healthcare services are also important. Thus, investments in healthcare infrastructure, reforms and universal health coverage are much needed. Addressing these areas will contribute to India's overall development and well-being.

It's important to improve the quality of education, ensure equitable access and align skill development with industry requirements. Gender equality remains a priority, with a focus on empowering women and providing equal opportunities. Social and political reforms are needed to strengthen governance, reduce corruption, enhance transparency, uphold the rule of law, protect human rights and ensure social justice. Addressing these areas will contribute greatly towards India's inclusive and sustainable development.

Defining HDI

The Human Development Index (HDI) is a composite measure developed by the UNDP to assess and compare human development across countries. It provides a comprehensive view of development beyond economic indicators and allows for cross-country comparisons. The HDI considers multiple dimensions of development to provide a more holistic understanding of human well-being.

It considers three dimensions: health (measured by life expectancy), education (measured by mean and expected years of schooling) and the standard of living. The Human Development Index (HDI) is determined by considering four indicators: life expectancy at birth, mean years of schooling, expected years of schooling and the Gross National Income (GNI) per capita. It takes into account: health, education and standard of living indicators. Each dimension is measured on a scale of 0 to 1, with 1 representing the highest level of development. The HDI provides a holistic view of development and is a valuable tool for monitoring progress and identifying areas for improvement. India's latest Human Development Index (HDI) rank is 131 out of 188 countries. This rank has been maintained from the previous year's report, with a score of 0.645 based on the factors considered in the HDI calculation.

How can India improve its HDI by 2050?

India faces the challenge of achieving a position among the top 25 countries with the highest Human Development Index (HDI), but it is not an impossible goal. The HDI considers factors like life expectancy, education and income to assess human development. India's progress in these areas will be crucial for improving its HDI ranking. While

India has made advancements in the above-mentioned areas, it still needs to address income inequality; improve access to education and healthcare and promote social inclusion, sustainable development practices, technological capabilities and governance to advance overall human development.

To attain a top-25 HDI ranking, India must prioritize policies and initiatives that foster inclusive growth, reduce disparities and enhance the well-being of its citizens. This entails investing in education, healthcare, infrastructure and sustainable development. Targeted interventions to uplift marginalized communities are also crucial. By focusing on these areas, India can make progress towards achieving its goal.

How can we inculcate a positive mind-set among our youth and society?

To promote positive social psychology in India, efforts should be made to engage citizens—especially the youth—in nationwide positive psychology programs by leveraging social media platforms. Encouraging and recognizing talent by providing scholarships, grants, mentorship programs and opportunities will foster a positive outlook. Cultivating a supportive mind-set by celebrating achievements and offering encouragement contributes to a more optimistic and supportive social environment. Implementing these strategies can help nurture positive social psychology in India.

Cultivating a positive mind-set among the Indian youth is essential for personal growth and national progress. Strategies include prioritizing emotional intelligence and life skills in education, promoting role models and mentorship, encouraging entrepreneurship and innovation, supporting sports and extracurricular activities and fostering digital literacy and responsible media consumption. Collective efforts from the government, educational institutions, families and communities are required to nurture a positive youth and society. Providing quality education, skill-development programs and mentorship initiatives will empower the youth to a great extent. Promoting emotional well-being, community service, positive role models, media and digital literacy, safe and inclusive spaces, civic engagement and family support are crucial for fostering a positive society in India. These strategies contribute to the holistic development of youth and create an environment that is conducive to positivity and progress.

Thus, fostering positive social psychology in India necessitates engaging citizens, particularly the youth, through a comprehensive program that harnesses the power of social media, promotes and rewards talent and also cultivates a supportive mind-set. By collectively embracing positivity and fostering a spirit of cooperation, India can create an environment that nurtures personal growth, resilience and well-being. This inclusive approach will bridge gaps, empower individuals and contribute to the nation's progress.

How can India become a Developed Nation?

To promote India's development and achieve higher human development, several key strategies should be pursued:

1. Strengthening institutions, improving governance and ensuring transparency and accountability are crucial for attracting investments and creating an enabling environment.

2. Promoting gender equality, social inclusion and addressing disparities will contribute to a more equitable society.

3. Prioritizing healthcare infrastructure, sanitation and preventive measures will promote better health outcomes.

4. Bridging the digital divide and fostering innovation and entrepreneurship will drive economic growth and technological advancements.

5. Engaging in international cooperation and partnerships for sustainable development will facilitate progress and global recognition.

What India needs to learn from the best practices of Developed Nations?

India can learn from the best practices of developed nations to enhance its development efforts. Some of the tactics that India can use are listed below

1. Investing in education by emphasizing research, innovation, teacher training and fostering a culture of lifelong learning can improve the quality of education.

2. Adopting best practices from developed countries in healthcare systems—including preventive care, universal access to healthcare and robust public health infrastructure—can further enhance the well-being of the population. These measures can contribute to India's progress and development.

3. Implementing sustainable development practiced in developed countries can help address environmental challenges, promote renewable-energy adoption and mitigate climate-change effects.

4. Studying comprehensive social-welfare systems of developed nations can advance the design and implementation of effective programs to reduce inequality, alleviate poverty and support vulnerable populations.

5. Focusing on good governance, transparency and citizen participation can help reduce corruption, streamline bureaucracy and promote accountability in decision-making processes.

6. Leveraging the experience in innovation and technology can help India foster an ecosystem of innovation, promote entrepreneurship and harness the power of technology for sustainable growth.

7. Studying the planning, implementation and maintenance of infrastructure projects in developed nations can assist India in improving connectivity, efficiency and quality of life through well-developed transportation, communication and basic amenities. India should adopt the best practices in urban planning from developed nations which can help India address the challenges of rapid urbanization by implementing smart city initiatives, efficient public transportation systems and affordable housing options.

8. By studying the practices of developed nations in environmental conservation, waste management and pollution control, India can find ways to balance economic development with environmental sustainability.

9. India should engage in understanding how developed nations promote social cohesion, inclusivity and equal opportunities which can help better address social disparities, discrimination and marginalization, thus fostering social harmony and integration.

To become a global leader by 2050, India should focus on strategies such as economic growth, global partnerships, sustainable development, knowledge and skill development, cultural diplomacy, humanitarian aid, talent pool nurturing, digital transformation, institution strengthening and youth empowerment. These strategies will not only position India as a key player on the global stage but also contribute to its overall development and lead to higher Human Development Index (HDI) rankings. Achieving these goals requires long-term commitment, collaboration and active citizen participation.

India Evolving as a Geopolitical Pivot

(A case study done by the author while studying at the Geneva School of Diplomacy and International Relations, Switzerland, from February to May 2023)

Executive Summary

India has the potential to become a global leader through its economic expansion, military strength and diplomatic reach. India has made significant progress in its economy, renewable-energy sector and military spending—becoming the world's largest arms importer between 2018 and 2022. Its foreign policy is focused on building strong economic, strategic and cultural ties with other countries while maintaining non-alignment. India aims to offset China's influence by increasing its ties with both the Global South and the West. India's relationships with global superpowers such as the US, China, Russia and the European Union are evolving, as impacted by economic interests, security concerns and geopolitical considerations. India can lead the Global South and create an international system that reflects the interests of developing countries.

India: Economic Superpower by 2050

Since the nineties, India's economy has risen dramatically as a result of several economic reforms. Despite issues such as the global economic slowdown, unemployment and the effects of demonetization, **India's GDP grew at an approximately 7% annual rate from 2014 to 2019** due to factors such as the expansion of the services sector, a concentration on exports and infrastructure investment. On April 11, 2023, the International Monetary Fund (IMF) released its latest World Economic Outlook report, anticipating 5.9 per cent growth in the current fiscal year, making India the world's fastest-growing economy. Nonetheless, the organization warned that disruptions in the financial system could harm the global economy as a whole. According to the IMF assessment, despite considerable hurdles—such as financial sector turbulence, inflationary pressures, the repercussions of the Russia–Ukraine war and the lingering impact of the Covid-19 outbreak over the previous three years—India will be the world's fastest-growing economy. According to an IVCA–Bain & Co estimate, **India developed 23 unicorns (privately held start-up businesses worth $1 billion or more) in 2022,** in comparison to China which created 11 such start-ups. India has surpassed China in terms of the number of unicorns created for the second year in a row. **The total number of unicorns valued at \$1 billion in India has now reached 96**.

Several programs, notably the 'Make in India' campaign and the 'Digital India' initiative, were enacted by the government to stimulate manufacturing, increase investment and reduce inflation. The country's renewable-energy sector and sustainable economic development are predicted to propel it to the world's second-largest economy by 2050. **In 2019, Standard Chartered reported that by 2030 India's economy will be second in the world with \$ 46.3 trillion,** while China will be on top at \$64.2 trillion. With over 1.4 billion people, India has surpassed China to become the most populous country, accounting for nearly **18 % of the total world population, with a median age of 28.4 years**. Thus, India is younger than China, which has a median age of 38 years. The demographic dividend in India refers to the country's young population, which is predicted to increase demand and attract foreign investment. This is because a young population is usually connected with a large and increasing consumer market as well as a productive workforce.

The increasing digitization of India's economy has increased in entrepreneurship, with more start-ups being formed and more venture capital investment spent on these start-ups. This tendency is likely to continue, boosting **India's growth and potential as an economic superpower**. Overall, these elements are considered to be critical in propelling India's economic growth and positioning it as a prominent player in the global economy. The move to renewable-energy sources in India is considered a driver of economic progress. Technological advancements—particularly in solar power—are likely to result in a huge decrease in the cost of green power, making it an appealing alternative for businesses and households. Indian Billionaire, Gautam Adani, estimates that India would **add a trillion dollars to its GDP every 12 to 18 months over the next decade,** making it a \$30 trillion economy with a \$45 trillion stock market value by 2050

Indian Defence Forces safeguarding the Indian Ocean

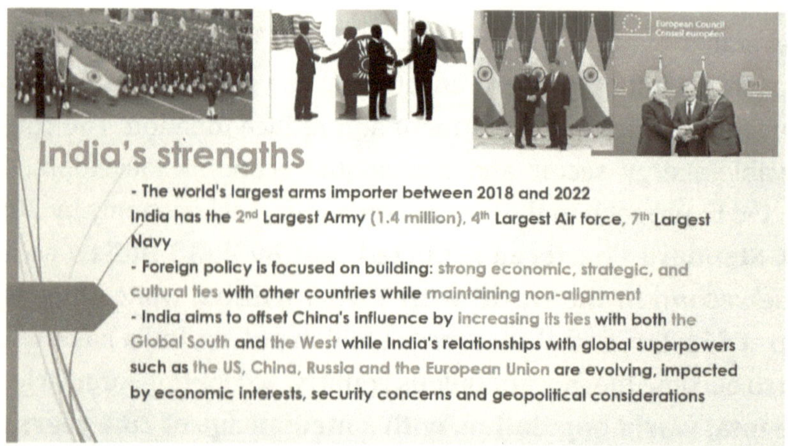

From 2018 to 2022, **India remained the world's largest arms+ importer**—owing to tensions with Pakistan and China—and its military spending has surged as a result. India also increased its investments in space technology and the modernization of its military capabilities. India aims to build a **200-ship Navy** by 2027 to counter Chinese influence in the Indian Ocean Region, which is a major commercial and trade hub that faces security threats such as piracy, terrorism, territory conflicts and geopolitical issues.

The Indian Ocean region's **'Security and Progress for All in the Region' (SAGAR)** policy aims to improve regional security and economic prosperity through various initiatives such as defending India's mainland and islands, promoting economic and security cooperation with maritime neighbours and encouraging collective action for peace and security. The policy also emphasizes sustainable growth and the establishment of trust and transparency with other states in the region. **SAGAR is a significant component of India's foreign policy and regional strategy for the Indian Ocean** and includes initiatives such as Sagarmala and Project Mausam.

Foreign Policy of India: Building Bridges between North-South and East-West

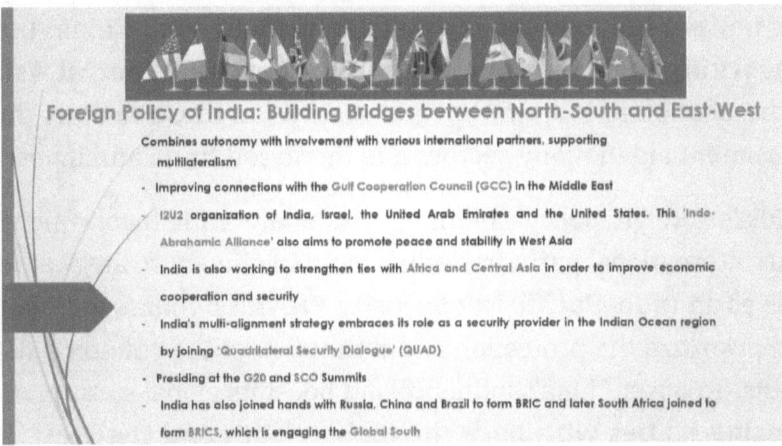

While staying non-aligned, India's foreign policy prioritizes strong economic, strategic and cultural ties with countries. It prioritizes collaboration with smaller neighbours and interaction with all countries, while also supporting multilateralism and improving connections with the **Gulf Cooperation Council (GCC)** in the Middle East. The '**I2U2**' organization—comprised of India, Israel, the United Arab Emirates and the United States—aspires to use its members' innovation and entrepreneurship to address global concerns such as water, energy, transportation, space, health and food security.

The proposed **'Indo–Abrahamic Alliance'** also aims to promote peace and stability in West Asia. Due to boundary issues and economic competition, the concept of multi-alignment entails interacting with major powers but keeping distinct connections with China. **India is also working to strengthen ties with Africa and Central Asia**—to improve economic cooperation and security in those regions through development aid in many sectors and increased trade and investment.

India's foreign policy combines autonomy with involvement with various international partners. India's multi-alignment strategy embraces its role as an **Indo–Pacific Net Security Provider.** India's foreign policy would prioritize the protection and promotion of the country's national interests. To offset China's influence and boost its global stature, **India is increasing its ties with both the Global South and the West.** India's expanding economy has allowed it to invest in poorer countries, but this assistance is not simply altruistic. Geopolitical issues propel India, especially its resistance towards China's dominance in the global south. Japan shares India's concerns about China's regional dominance and collaborates with it in the Indian Ocean region as part of the **'Quadrilateral Security Dialogue' (Quad)** along with the US and Australia.

The G20 & SCO Presidency of India in 2023

India is preparing to host the **G-20 meeting in September 2023**, during which all G-20 leaders will sign the Leaders' Declaration. The theme of India's presidency will be 'Vasudhaiva Kutumbakam' or '**One Earth, One Family, One Future**', highlighting the value of all life and its interconnectedness on Earth and beyond the universe, as well as environmentally sustainable and responsible decisions. India will prioritize green development; climate finance; LiFE (Lifestyle for Environment); rapid, inclusive and resilient growth; SDG acceleration; technological transformation; the 21st-century multilateral institutions and women-led development. The seminars will be held in over 50 places across the country, displaying India's rich cultural history.

The next **Shanghai Cooperation Organization (SCO) Summit**, which India will host in July 2023, **would have far-reaching ramifications for India's regional and global engagement.** As a full-fledged member of the SCO, India may advocate for its regional interests including the improvement of connectivity with the **Central Asian Republics (CARs)**, which is comprised of 6 countries namely Kazakhstan, Kyrgyz Republic, Tajikistan, Turkmenistan and Uzbekistan. India's economic diplomacy in the SCO aims to increase its influence in the CARs markets, which have enormous trade and investment possibilities. India's trade in CARs is growing, but there is still potential for improvement. India has proposed the development of a special working group on innovation and start-ups as well as a working group on traditional medicine and partnership to benefit micro, small and medium-sized companies. India also plans to increase tourism and begin a more extensive discussion of a trade and investment development agenda. In this regard, India has already taken several steps including the International North–South Transport Corridor and the Chabahar port project.

Finally, India's hosting of the SCO Summit in 2023 provides an important opportunity for India to strengthen its regional and global participation. To attain the full potential of its SCO membership, India must overcome various obstacles, but with careful diplomacy and strategic engagement it may benefit from the opportunities given by the SCO platform. The SCO membership also provides India with a platform **for positive engagement with Pakistan and China** as well as an alternative regional forum for handling Afghanistan's predicament.

India's engagement with Powerful Nations (with the US, EU, Russia, China, Japan and Australia)

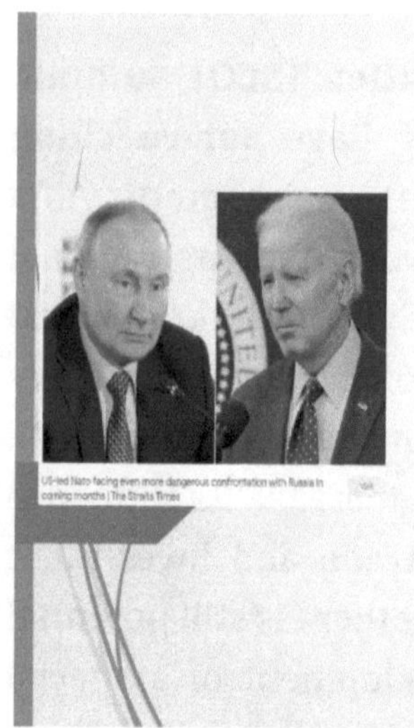

The West is at a Crossroad now as there is a growing concern among European leaders about the USA's status as the **Western World's leader**. Concerns have been raised regarding the commitment of the US towards NATO, its relations with Russia and the handling of topics such as climate change and immigration. These concerns have called into question the future of the Trans–Atlantic Partnership and the USA's role as a global leader.

India's diplomatic relationship with the global superpowers—the **United States, China, Russia and the European Union (EU)**—has evolved and is impacted by a variety of factors such as economic interests, security concerns and geopolitical considerations. The **India–US relationship**, in particular, is distinguished by a strong strategic partnership founded on shared democratic ideals and a rising convergence on a wide range of topics including commerce, defence, education, science and technology and cyber security among others. People-to-people interaction and political backing in both countries add to the relationship's strength.

India's potential as a partner for the US is again emphasized particularly in light of concerns about China's ascent. India, with its huge population and rapid economic growth, is an appealing option for supply chains, innovation centres and joint ventures. The possibility of establishing a **technology corridor between India and the United States is addressed**, which would further position **India as a worldwide technological leader** while also creating a secure supply chain.

Furthermore, **India and the EU** have a similar commitment to safeguarding and advancing human rights and establishing a global order based on rules, effective multilateralism, long-term growth and free trade. The volume of commerce in commodities and services, foreign investment and the presence of European enterprises in India all contribute to the importance of India's trading connection with the European Union. **With regular summits and ministerial meetings** focused on security and foreign policy consultations, **India and the European Union's strategic cooperation has become stronger over tie.**

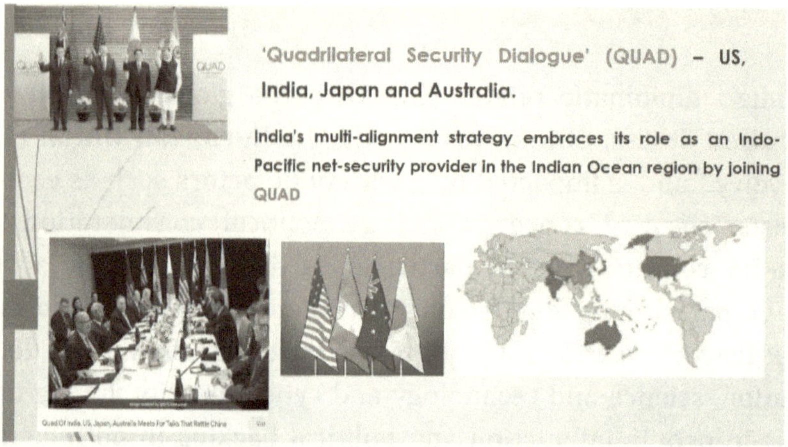

India has made several efforts to enhance diplomatic ties with other countries, which include the Indian Prime Minister's frequent trips abroad since taking office in 2014. These trips resulted in several positive consequences **including improved economic relations, more foreign investment and expanded strategic alliances.** Some of India's notable foreign policy achievements include signing the Paris Agreement; forming the International Solar Alliance and establishing the **Quad with the United States, Japan and Australia.** At the time of these visits, India's leadership in digital technology and Industry 4.0 was on display, highlighting India's position as a major participant in the industry.

The Russia-India-China (RIC) Triangular Relationship

Because of shifting geopolitical realities, **India's relationship with Russia and China**, sometimes known as the **RIC Triangle,** has evolved. While India and Russia have a long history of strategic collaboration, changes in the global order have had an impact on their relationship. India's efforts to diversify its weapon suppliers have resulted in a reduction in Russian arms delivery, although the two countries continue to engage in defence, energy, nuclear energy, connectivity and Covid-19 activities. **Russia's foreign policy prioritizes** expanding connections with friendly countries and **developing partnerships with China and India**, all the while viewing the United States as its greatest threat.

Meanwhile, as a result of the China–US rivalry the **China–Russia relationship has grown closer,** and they have explored collaboration in agriculture, metals, energy, e-commerce, pharmaceuticals and emerging technology. Their collaboration, however, has limitations as they have not established an anti-Western front yet. **The RIC trio has the potential to reform the international system and maintain Asian stability**, but, in comparison to other multilateral organizations, they are yet to implement real cooperation programs and institutional building.

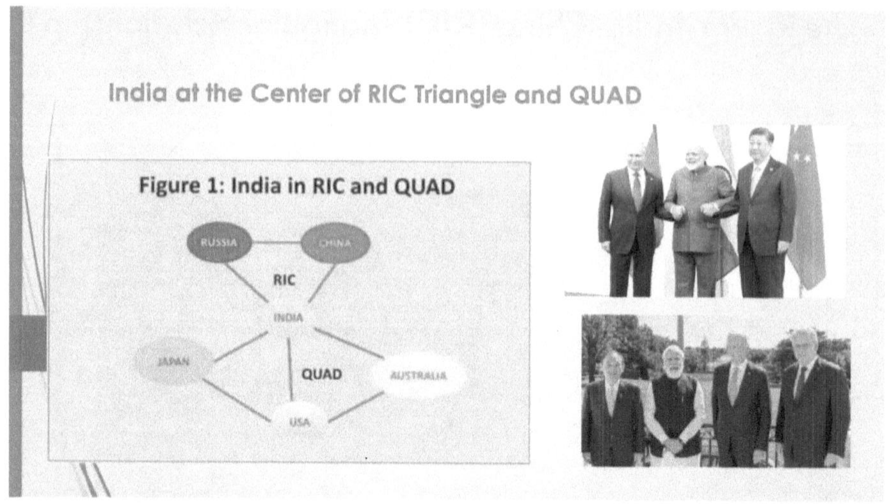

The establishment of a successful trilateral RIC institution might contribute to the establishment of an inclusive and **long-term Asian security cooperation structure**, allowing the **RIC to address underlying concerns between India and China while also contributing to regional peace and development.** India has several challenges including a lack of direct land connectivity, growing Russia-China convergence and conflicts over the **Belt and Road** Initiative. To overcome these challenges, India must prioritize its relations with China—with which it shares geopolitical and economic interests—while also engaging with Russia, a key player in the region and China's close ally.

Overall, cooperation between India, Russia and China might benefit all parties while also improving regional stability. Despite significant barriers to cooperation, such as geopolitical rivalries, economic inequalities and security concerns, **the RIC Triangle has a significant potential to become a leading economic force by 2030—given its massive population, local markets, infrastructure investment,** expanding middle class and technological breakthroughs.

India's relationships with the Global South and other countries

India organized the '**Voice of Global South Summit**' in January 2023 which is emerging to become a major voice in international politics for the global south. India, being the **world's largest democracy**, has a varied population and economy and a long history of working for the rights and interests of developing countries. India's recent economic and technological gains have provided it with a platform to advocate for the global south—particularly in trade, climate change and multilateralism.

India's participation in the **International Solar Alliance and the Global South–South Development Expo** has demonstrated its commitment to promoting sustainable development in the global south. Due to its diverse society and economy, democratic principles and history of campaigning for impoverished countries, India is best positioned **to lead the global south in creating an international system** that best represents the needs and interests of the developing world.

India's oil diplomacy and efforts to transition to natural energy sources

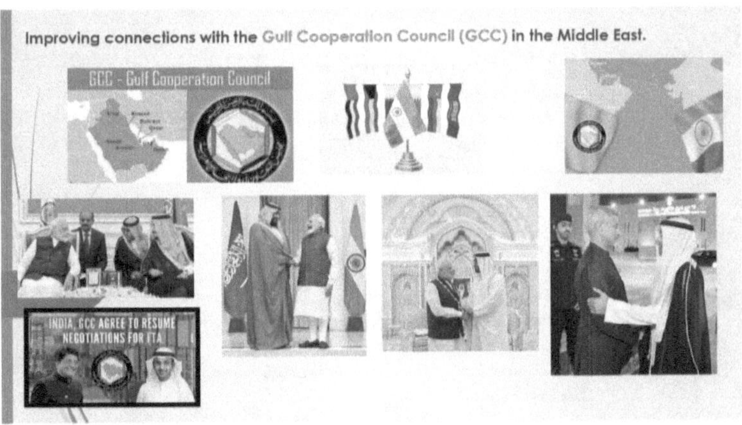

Oil diplomacy has been used by India to manage global energy market disruptions caused by the COVID-19 epidemic and geopolitical conflicts. India, the world's third-largest energy importer, has utilized its trade deficit as a geopolitical tool to meet its energy requirements. **India has developed as an important market for several countries—including the United States, Russia, Latin America and Africa—with a petroleum refining capacity** similar to that of several European countries combined. India's energy trade with the United States has increased dramatically in recent years, with oil and gas being the primary drivers. Since 2021, **India has been the largest buyer of US crude oil, and the US is India's fifth-largest exporter of refined petroleum.** Moreover, **despite Western sanctions on Russia and G7 price limitations, India has become the second-largest importer of Russian petroleum since March 2022.**

India plans to achieve energy independence by 2047 by switching from fossil fuels to indigenous energy sources. The **Indian government has launched several programs to promote renewable-energy sources** including the National Policy on Biofuels and the Ethanol Blended Petrol Program; it also plans on providing incentives for green hydrogen generation.

India can become a global power

India has the capacity to become a Global Leader

- India has the capacity to become a global leader in the future as a result of its **rich history, massive population, strategic location and rapid economic expansion**
- India's **new foreign policy strategy aspires to position it at the center of the Eurasian continent,** allowing it to play a vital role in influencing global politics and economy in the future
- India is preparing to host the **G-20 and SCO summits** as it overtakes China as the world's most populous country
- India's new foreign policy approach puts it as a prominent role in the **BRICS, SCO, QUAD and Global South organizations,** and it is heavily investing in space technology and modernizing its military forces
- As a counterbalance to China, the **United States will continue to support India's development**

India can become a global leader in the future as a result of its **rich history, massive population, strategic location and rapid economic expansion**. India's **new foreign policy strategy aspires to position it at the centre of the Eurasian continent,** allowing it to play a vital role in influencing global politics and economy in the future. However, India continues to face enormous difficulties that could stymie its development to superpower status such as poverty, inequality, corruption and geopolitical disputes with neighbouring countries. To solve these concerns, India is aggressively investing in space technology and growing its military capabilities as well as forming strategic alliances with other countries. To realize its full potential as a superpower, India must focus on energy and food grain self-sufficiency as well as commercializing the space industry and employing resources more efficiently through economic policies. While India's long-term growth prospects are promising, the country must overcome these obstacles if it is to reach its full potential as a global leader by 2040.

Significant years ahead: India's global significance is constantly growing as it is emerging as a geopolitical pivot in Eurasia. India is preparing to host the G-20 and SCO summits as it overtakes China as the world's most populous country. India's new foreign policy approach allows the country to play prominent roles in the **BRICS, SCO, Quad and the Global South organizations**; the country is also heavily investing in space technology and modernizing its military forces.

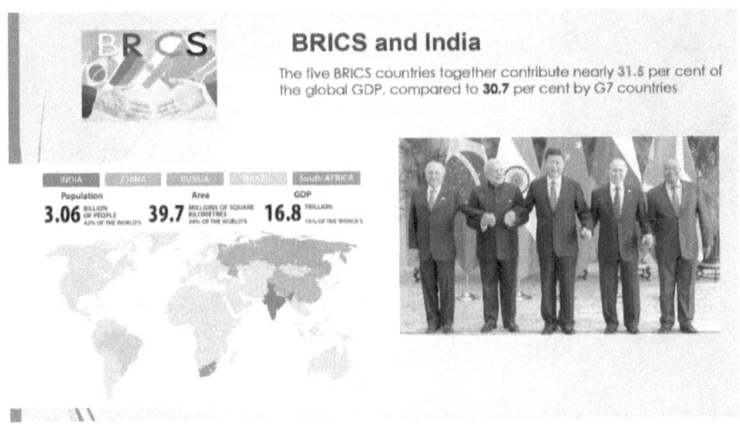

Through programs such as the **Quadrilateral Security Dialogue (Quad)**, India has been working on strategic ties with other countries. China will be India's primary foreign policy problem in 2023, as it has constantly disregarded border agreements in its quest to push into the Indian Territory. India's defence capabilities will take time to catch up with those of China. Despite such problems, India's relationship with the US and Europe will continue to develop since both countries strive to control China: this common interest will help maintain their strategic collaboration. As a counterbalance to China, the United States will continue to support India's development.

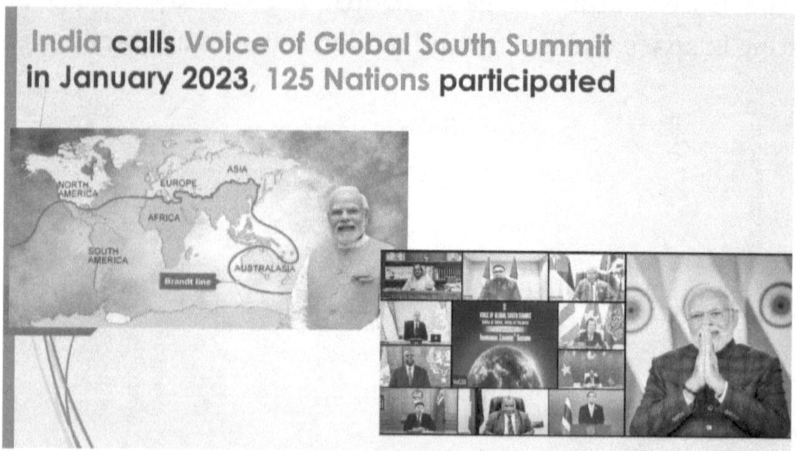

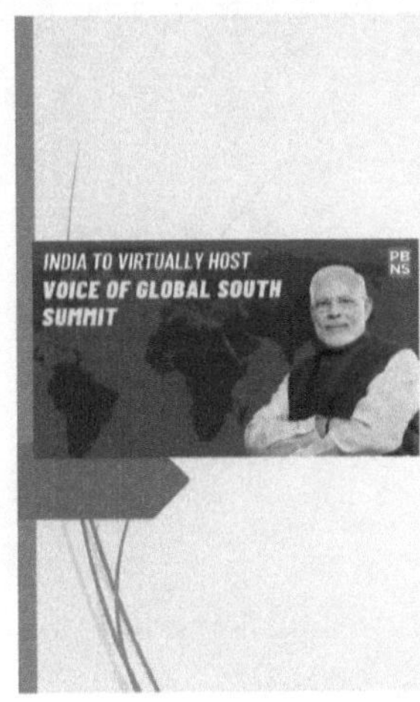

India's relationships with the Global South and other countries

India's relationships with the Global South and other countries

India organized the '**Voice of Global South Summit**' in January 2023, which is emerging to be a major voice in international politics for the global south. India, being the **world's largest democracy**.

India's participation in the **International Solar Alliance and the Global South-South Development Expo** have demonstrated its commitment to promoting sustainable development in the global south.

Due to its diverse society and economy, democratic principles and history of campaigning for impoverished countries.
India is best positioned **to lead the global south in creating the international system** to represent the needs and interests of the developing world.

Conclusion

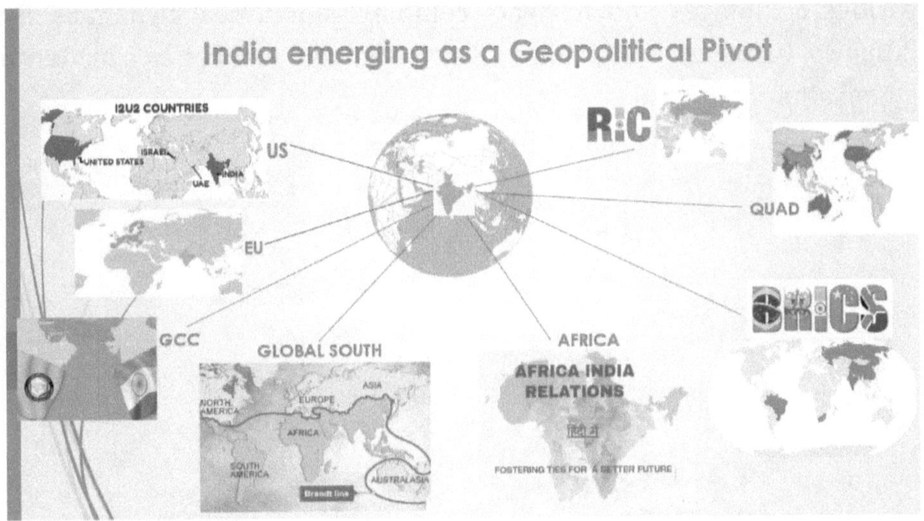

India's ambition to establish itself as a major global actor through multi-alignment foreign policies is admirable. India aspires to serve as a bridge between diverse regions, balancing the interests of developed countries with those of the developing world, particularly in terms of climate-financing objectives. By holding the G-20 presidency and welcoming Eurasian leaders, India aims to exert its influence on the global agenda. However, India faces numerous challenges on both domestic and foreign fronts. Poverty and inequality remain to be significant concerns, but India must also address social issues such as gender inequality and discrimination. In addition to this, India faces geopolitical tensions with Pakistan and China, and it has to navigate the **'great power'** competition—especially between the US and China. Balancing partnerships with different countries and avoiding getting caught up in the US–China rivalry is crucial. India also faces regional challenges such as the on-going conflict in Afghanistan and the instability in its neighbourhood: particularly in Pakistan and the disputed territory of Jammu and Kashmir. These issues can potentially derail India's efforts to become a major global player and hence they must be addressed with care. In conclusion, while India has the potential to become a prominent global player, it must also address various challenges and navigate complex geopolitical dynamics. By doing so, India can fully realize its potential and emerge as a leader in global affairs.

21 Visions for a Developed India by 2050

Invest in Quality Education

'The Economic Survey, 2022-23, shows that while student enrolment is higher, school-level infrastructure is better and there are more teachers to boot, the total expenditure (combined states and Centre) on education as a percentage of GDP had stayed stagnant at 2.9% since 2019, and is only marginally up from 2.8% in FY16...Several policy prescriptions on education, including the new National Education Policy, 2020, have reiterated the need to push up public investment in the sector to 6% of GDP'.

—The Economic Times, February 2nd, 2023.

Introduction

Investment in high-quality education is vital for the advancement and well-being of any country. It acts as a catalyst for positive societal transformations, poverty eradication and economic growth. For India to realize its aspirations of becoming a developed nation, it must prioritize education reforms, enhance access to quality education and promote skill development. This section aims to underscore the significance of investing in quality education, examine the challenges faced by the Indian education system and propose potential strategies to cultivate a knowledgeable and skilled workforce capable of propelling India towards development and prosperity.

In the specific context of India, giving considerable importance to investments in quality education holds immense value. With its vast and diverse population, ensuring equal access to quality education for all is crucial to unlock the nation's full potential. By equipping its citizens with relevant knowledge and skills, India can bridge gaps in income inequality, gender disparities and socio-economic divisions that exist within its society. By providing equitable educational opportunities and empowering individuals, India can pave the way for a more inclusive and prosperous future.

What is Quality Education?

Quality education plays a pivotal role in personal growth, professional success and social development. It encompasses more than just subject knowledge and emphasizes critical thinking, problem-solving, communication and adaptability skills. When individuals receive a high-quality education, they are better equipped to contribute to both economic growth and societal advancement. Education has the power to shape the future by enabling individuals to excel in their chosen fields and make positive impacts within their communities.

A well-educated workforce fuels innovation, reduces disparities and fosters social cohesion. Furthermore, quality education instils values such as empathy and respect for diversity—nurturing responsible citizens who actively engage in their communities. Ultimately, it serves as the fundamental foundation for individual and societal progress—empowering individuals, promoting economic growth and fostering social harmony and responsible citizenship.

The Present State of the Indian Education System and the Challenges before it

The Indian education system has made progress in improving access to education, especially at the primary level. However, concerns about the quality of education persist, with significant disparities between urban and rural areas. The heavy emphasis on high-stakes exams fosters a culture of memorization and intense competition among students. While there are numerous universities and colleges in India, the quality of higher education varies widely. Skill development and vocational education are becoming more important to meet the demands of the job market. The integration of technology in education is advancing, though challenges in access and connectivity remain. Insufficient infrastructure, unequal access, out-dated curriculum, teacher shortages and inadequate investment in research and development are major obstacles that hinder the provision of quality education and skill development. Collaborative efforts from various stakeholders are needed to address these issues and promote equitable access, updated curricula, well-prepared teachers and increased investment in research and development. Overcoming these challenges can help establish a strong and inclusive foundation for future generations in India.

Measures to overcome these challenges

To ensure quality education in India, several key reforms and measures need to be implemented. These include updating the curriculum to focus on critical thinking and practical skills, improving educational infrastructure in rural and marginalized areas and enhancing access to education for girls and marginalized communities. Teacher training and professional development are important to improve the quality of teaching, while technology integration can make learning more engaging and accessible. Collaborating with the private sector, investing in early childhood education and offering skill-development programs will also contribute to a better education system. Providing scholarships and financial assistance to deserving students and implementing effective assessments and monitoring mechanisms are vital steps in ensuring quality education. Furthermore, encouraging parent and community engagement, as well as promoting research and innovation in education, will further enhance the overall quality of the educational system in India. By prioritizing these reforms, India can empower its population, reduce disparities and foster economic and social growth through access to quality education.

10 Steps that India can undertake to guarantee a high standard of education for its students

To ensure the provision of quality education for students in India, several strategies can be employed across different levels. Here are some fundamental steps that can be taken:

1. **Enhancing Teacher Training:** It is vital to improve the quality of teachers. This can be achieved through comprehensive and continuous professional development programs that focus on pedagogical techniques, subject knowledge and classroom management. Such initiatives can significantly enhance the overall quality of education.

2. **Revamping the Curriculum:** Regularly reviewing and updating the curriculum to align with global standards and industry requirements is crucial. The curriculum should emphasize critical thinking, problem-solving, creativity and practical skill development, moving away from a heavy emphasis on rote memorization.

3. **Developing Infrastructure:** Ensuring that schools have adequate infrastructure and

4. **Essential Resources:** This includes well-equipped classrooms, libraries, science laboratories and computer facilities. In addition to these, accessible and safe school buildings with amenities like clean drinking water and sanitation facilities are vital components.

5. **Integrating Technology:** Leveraging technology can enhance the learning experience. Providing students and teachers with access to digital resources, interactive educational tools and

online learning platforms can expand their knowledge base and foster independent learning.

6. **Promoting Equity and Inclusion:** Addressing educational disparities among different regions, socio-economic backgrounds and gender is of utmost importance. Scholarships, subsidies and special programs can be implemented to ensure that students from marginalized communities have equal opportunities to access quality education.

7. **Ensuring Assessment and Accountability:** Implementing a robust system of continuous evaluation and standardized assessments can help monitor student progress and identify areas for improvement. Furthermore, holding educational institutions accountable for maintaining quality standards through regular inspections and evaluations is crucial.

8. **Encouraging Parent and Community Engagement:** Promoting parental involvement and community participation in education can have a positive impact. Conducting workshops, organizing parent–teacher meetings and involving community members in school activities can foster a supportive and conducive learning environment.

9. **Fostering Collaboration and Partnerships:** Collaboration between government bodies, educational institutions, non-governmental organizations and private entities can lead to innovative solutions and resource sharing. Public–private partnerships can help bridge gaps in funding and infrastructure development.

10. **Promoting Research and Innovation:** Encouraging research and innovation in the education sector can drive improvements. Supporting educational research institutions, promoting research-based teaching practices and adopting evidence-based policies can contribute to enhancing the education system.

11. **Continuous Monitoring and Evaluation:** Regularly monitoring and evaluating the effectiveness of the implemented measures is crucial. This process helps identify areas that require further improvement and enables policymakers to make informed decisions based on evidence.

It is important to acknowledge that implementing these measures requires a comprehensive approach involving government initiatives, community participation and a sustained commitment to the development of the education system.

Conclusion

In conclusion, making substantial investments in quality education is of utmost importance for India's development and progress. By giving priority to education reforms, ensuring widespread access to education and nurturing skill development, India can cultivate a well-informed workforce that will drive economic growth and societal advancement. Overcoming challenges will require focusing on infrastructure development, enhancing teacher training, integrating technology and fostering inclusive education. The collaborative efforts of the government, educators, parents and the community are crucial in achieving these goals. With a resolute commitment to quality education, India can empower its citizens, diminish inequality and strive for global leadership by the year 2050.

VISION 2

Foster Innovation and Research

"India climbed six notches to 40th position in the Global Innovation Index, 2022, on account of improvement in several parameters, according to a report by the Geneva-based World Intellectual Property Organization (WIPO). Switzerland, the United States, Sweden, the United Kingdom and the Netherlands are the world's most-innovative economies, according to WIPO's 2022 Global Innovation Index (GII), with China on the threshold of the top 10. Other emerging economies are also showing consistently strong performances including India and Turkey, both of which have entered the top 40 for the first time."

—*Business Today, Sep 30th, 2022*

Introduction

To achieve its objective of becoming a developed nation, India must prioritize innovation and research. This necessitates investing in research and development (R&D), fostering an environment conducive to innovation and supporting entrepreneurship. These efforts will enable India to unlock its potential, harness the creative abilities of its citizens and effectively address the critical challenges it faces.

By recognizing the importance of innovation and research, India can unlock its full potential and lay the foundation for its development journey. India can harness the creative talents of its people to effectively tackle pressing national challenges by increasing R&D investments, cultivating an ecosystem that fosters innovation and providing support for entrepreneurs. Innovation and research serve as catalysts for progress and can propel India forward in its quest to become a developed nation.

Defining Innovation and Research

Innovation encompasses the introduction of original concepts, methodologies, products or services that result in notable improvements or progress. It involves utilizing creativity, knowledge and problem-solving skills to develop inventive solutions that address existing problems or meet emerging needs.

Research is a systematic process that aims to generate new knowledge and insights by collecting, analyzing and interpreting data on a specific subject across various fields. It plays a crucial role in laying the foundation for innovation. Innovation, in turn, applies the findings of research in practical ways. Together, research and innovation drive societal progress and economic well-being by creating novel products, services and processes that improve productivity, quality of life and address social issues. To remain at the forefront of technological advancements and scientific breakthroughs, countries must nurture an innovative culture and allocate resources to support research and development.

The Present State of Innovation and Research in India and the Challenges before it

The current state of innovation and research in India is characterized by impressive accomplishments and promising prospects, along with persistent obstacles. India has made notable advancements in technology, healthcare, agriculture and space exploration. The technology sector has experienced rapid growth, with Indian companies demonstrating exceptional innovation. India is renowned for its expertise in generic drug manufacturing, medical research in healthcare, innovative practices in agriculture and notable achievements in space exploration. The country's start-up ecosystem is also vibrant and disruptive.

India has made strides in innovation and research, and this is evident in its thriving start-up ecosystem and talented pool of scientists and entrepreneurs. However, challenges persist including the need for increased R&D investment, stronger industry–academia collaborations, regulatory improvements, better protection of intellectual property rights, improved funding access and enhanced skill development. By addressing these challenges, India can solidify its position as a global frontrunner in innovation and research.

Measures to overcome these challenges

Measures such as increasing R&D funding, fostering collaboration between academia and industry, streamlining regulations, protecting intellectual property, enhancing funding options and investing in skill development are crucial for propelling India's progress in these areas. Tackling these challenges will attract global investments, drive economic growth and establish India as a leader in scientific and technological advancements worldwide.

10 Strategies by which India can foster innovation and research to progress towards becoming a developed nation:

The proposed measures aim to promote research and development (R&D) and innovation through increased investment, industry–academia collaborations, improved regulations, better access to funding and addressing skill gaps. Encouraging international collaboration can provide access to new ideas and resources. Creating a supportive ecosystem involves establishing incubation centres, innovation hubs and technology parks to foster risk-taking and learning from failures. Government support and policies should prioritize innovation and establish dedicated bodies and programs to overlook the same. Implementing these strategies will drive economic growth, address societal challenges and position India as a global leader in research and innovation.

1. **Promote a Culture of Innovation:** Create an ecosystem that encourages and rewards innovation. Foster a culture where creativity, risk-taking and experimentation are valued and supported. This can be achieved by recognizing and celebrating innovative achievements, providing incentives for research and development and fostering collaboration between academia, industry and government.

2. **Invest in Research and Development:** Increase investment in research and development (R&D) across various sectors. Allocate resources to research institutions, universities and laboratories to enhance their capabilities and infrastructure. Provide grants, funding and tax incentives to encourage both public and private entities to invest in R&D.

3. **Strengthen Research Institutions:** Enhance the capacity and quality of research institutions and universities by providing adequate funding, state-of-the-art facilities and research grants. Foster collaborations between academic institutions, industry and international research organizations to facilitate knowledge exchange and interdisciplinary research.

4. **Promote Industry–Academia Collaboration:** Encourage collaboration between academia and industry to bridge the gap between theoretical knowledge and practical application. Establish partnerships, joint research projects and technology transfer mechanisms to facilitate the translation of research findings into innovative products, services and solutions.

5. **Entrepreneurship and Start-up Support:** Foster an entrepreneurial ecosystem that supports the growth of start-ups and encourages innovative ideas. Provide access to funding, mentorship programs, incubation centres and regulatory support to nurture and scale innovative ventures. Promote the development of technology parks and innovation clusters to create a conducive environment for entrepreneurship.

6. **Intellectual Property Rights (IPR) Protection:** Strengthen intellectual property rights laws and enforcement mechanisms to protect the rights of innovators and creators. Create awareness about the importance of IPR and provide support for patent filing, licensing and commercialization of intellectual property.

7. **Collaboration with Global Research Networks:** Facilitate collaboration with global research networks, international institutions and universities to leverage global expertise, knowledge exchange and research partnerships. Encourage Indian researchers to participate in international conferences, workshops and collaborative projects.

8. **Promote STEM Education:** Strengthen the focus on science, technology, engineering and mathematics (STEM) education from an early stage. Introduce innovative pedagogical approaches and practical learning experiences to inspire and nurture young minds. Foster curiosity, critical thinking, problem-solving skills and creativity among students.

9. **Government Support and Policies:** Develop policies that incentivize and support innovation and research. Establish dedicated funding schemes, grants and tax incentives for research and innovation initiatives. Streamline regulatory processes and create a favourable business environment for research-oriented industries.

10. **Public Awareness and Engagement:** Create awareness among the general public about the importance of innovation and research for national development. Promote science popularization programs, public lectures and exhibitions to engage citizens and inspire young minds to pursue careers in research and innovation.

By adopting these strategies and fostering a culture of innovation and research, India can harness its intellectual capital, promote economic growth and propel the nation towards becoming a developed country.

Conclusion

To achieve its goal of becoming a developed nation by 2050, India needs to prioritize research and development (R&D) and foster a culture of innovation. This entails making significant investments in R&D infrastructure, promoting collaboration between academia and industry and formulating supportive policies. By strengthening its scientific and technological capabilities, India can stimulate economic growth and improve the standard of living. Collaboration between academia and industry is crucial for effectively translating research findings into practical applications. Supportive policies—including grants and tax incentives—will encourage investment in R&D and facilitate the commercialization of innovative ideas. Giving importance to STEM education from an early stage will nurture a skilled workforce capable of driving future innovation. By embracing research and innovation, India can position itself as a global leader, address societal challenges and achieve inclusive growth by 2050.

Enhance Infrastructure

Introduction

Infrastructure development plays a vital role in the progress and development of a nation. It forms the backbone of an economy, supporting various sectors and improving the quality of life for its citizens. For India to become a developed nation, enhancing infrastructure is crucial. This essay explores the importance of investing in robust infrastructure, the challenges faced by India in this regard and potential strategies to accelerate infrastructure development to support economic growth and improve the overall well-being of its people.

Defining Good Infrastructure

Good infrastructure refers to a well-planned, reliable and accessible system of physical and organizational elements that support a community or region. It includes efficient facilities and services that contribute to development, functionality and well-being. The key attributes include accessibility, safety, efficiency, capacity, sustainability, connectivity, innovation, inclusivity and adaptability. Such infrastructure fosters economic growth, improves quality of life and promotes overall progress.

Infrastructure development is a crucial driver of a country's economic growth and the well-being of its people. It offers numerous benefits including increased productivity, attracting investments, job creation and improved living standards. Every investment in infrastructure has a positive multiplier effect on the GDP. Infrastructure facilitates trade, expands market access, boosts competitiveness and attracts investments. It also creates jobs, supports industries and narrows down regional disparities. Furthermore, infrastructure development improves transportation, provides essential services and promotes social progress by ensuring access to healthcare, education and public facilities—fostering inclusivity. In summary, robust infrastructure plays a pivotal role in a country's overall development and progress.

The Present State of Indian Infrastructure and the Challenges before it

India's rapid economic growth and urbanization have led to a strong demand for robust infrastructure development. To support its economic expansion and become one of the world's largest economies by 2050, India has set ambitious goals and launched various initiatives. The Pradhan Mantri Gati Shakti National Master Plan aims to coordinate infrastructure projects for efficient connectivity, safety and sustainability. It emphasizes sustainable mobility solutions and streamlined clearance processes. Over the next 25 years, India has identified four key objectives to guide its infrastructure development, known as 'Amrit Kaal'. The National Infrastructure Pipeline (NIP) is another significant initiative focused on coordination, project preparation and attracting investments. These efforts aim to build world-class infrastructure and contribute to sustained economic growth, social development and improved quality of life for Indian citizens.

Infrastructure development in India encounters several challenges that require attention for successful and sustainable growth. These challenges include securing funding and investment, improving planning and coordination among government agencies, addressing land acquisition issues and streamlining the regulatory environment. To overcome these hurdles, India must adopt a comprehensive approach involving policy reforms, capacity building and stakeholder engagement. By addressing these challenges, India can promote infrastructure development, support economic growth and achieve its development goals.

Measures to Overcome Challenges:

To address infrastructure development challenges, India can implement key strategies such as strengthening funding mechanisms, streamlining regulatory processes, improving planning and coordination and fostering technology and innovation adoption. These strategies aim to enhance access to funding, simplify regulatory procedures, optimize resource allocation and promote the adoption of advanced technologies. By implementing these measures, India can overcome challenges, drive economic growth and improve infrastructure quality for its citizens. Furthermore, prioritizing sustainability and resilience; facilitating land acquisition and rehabilitation; promoting skill development and capacity building; enhancing public awareness and participation; strengthening monitoring and evaluation and fostering international collaboration are other crucial strategies that will help India promote sustainable and high-quality infrastructure development, ensuring its long-term success and economic progress.

10 Strategies by which India can enhance its infrastructure:

1. **Develop a Comprehensive and Long-Term Infrastructure Vision:** India needs a clear and long-term vision for infrastructure development that aligns with its economic goals and considers the diverse needs of different sectors and

regions. This will enable effective planning and prioritization of projects.

2. **Conduct a Thorough Infrastructure Needs Assessment:** A detailed assessment of infrastructure requirements is crucial to identify gaps and prioritize projects. This assessment should consider economic, social and environmental factors to address the most critical needs of the country.

3. **Ensure Policy Stability:** Creating a stable policy environment is essential to attract investments and instil confidence in infrastructure development. Establishing clear guidelines, consistent regulations and a long-term vision will provide certainty to investors and encourage their participation.

4. **Implement Effective Governance and Project Management:** Strengthening governance frameworks, enhancing transparency and ensuring efficient project management are key to minimizing delays, cost overruns and quality issues. Robust monitoring, streamlined approval processes and the use of technology can help achieve these goals.

5. **Foster Public–Private Partnerships:** Public–Private Partnerships (PPPs) can bring in private-sector expertise, investment and efficiency to infrastructure development. Encouraging partnerships between the public and private sectors will unlock additional resources and benefits from private-sector innovation. Transparent and fair frameworks must be established to protect public interests.

6. **Focus on Maintenance and Asset Management:** Emphasizing regular maintenance and effective asset management is vital for ensuring the longevity and efficiency of infrastructure assets. Neglecting maintenance can lead to premature deterioration and reduced service quality. Allocating resources and implementing robust maintenance practices are necessary for sustainable infrastructure development.

7. **Invest in Research and Development:** Allocating resources to research and development (R&D) in infrastructure is essential for promoting innovation, developing indigenous technologies and finding sustainable and cost-effective solutions. R&D investments can lead to the adoption of advanced construction techniques, improved materials and innovative infrastructure designs.

8. **Embrace Smart and Digital Technologies:** Integrating digital technologies, automation and smart solutions in infrastructure development can significantly enhance efficiency, connectivity and service delivery. Leveraging technologies like the Internet of Things (IoT), data analytics and artificial intelligence can optimize operations, improve resource management and enhance user experiences.

9. **Promote Sustainability and Resilience:** Incorporating sustainability and resilience principles into infrastructure projects is crucial for long-term development. By adopting green practices, promoting renewable-energy sources, incorporating climate-change adaptation measures and designing infrastructure to withstand natural disasters—India can build infrastructure that is environmentally friendly, resilient and able to withstand future challenges.

10. **Ensure Inclusive Infrastructure Development:** Prioritizing inclusive infrastructure development is essential to address the needs of all segments of society, including vulnerable communities. This involves ensuring accessibility, affordability and equitable distribution of infrastructure services. Projects should consider the specific requirements of marginalized groups, such as providing adequate transportation in remote areas or improving access to basic services in underserved regions.

By implementing these steps, India can enhance its infrastructure and make significant progress toward becoming a developed nation. However, it is important to recognize that infrastructure development is a long-term process that requires sustained commitment, collaboration and adaptability to evolving needs and technologies.

Conclusion

By the year 2050, India's infrastructure will witness significant advancements fuelled by strategic investments and innovative solutions. This development will address regional disparities by establishing dependable transportation networks, energy systems and digital connectivity throughout the nation. The progress will be supported by strong funding mechanisms, streamlined regulations and technological breakthroughs.

Emphasis will be placed on sustainability, energy efficiency, eco-friendly practices and adapting to climate change. Skill-development initiatives will cultivate a proficient workforce, and public involvement will ensure that infrastructure projects cater to local needs. Monitoring and evaluation systems will be implemented to track progress and maintain accountability. These comprehensive strategies will result in a resilient, inclusive and sustainable infrastructure in India by 2050, driving economic growth and enhancing the overall quality of life. As a result, India will emerge as a global leader, inspiring other nations in the 21ˢᵗ century.

Promote Sustainable Development

Introduction

Sustainable development is crucial for India's progress as it balances economic growth, social equity and environmental conservation. To ensure sustainable development, India should focus on improving water management systems, promoting education and awareness and investing in green technology and innovation. Implementing practices such as rainwater harvesting, watershed management and water recycling can enhance water security. Incorporating sustainability into school curricula and raising awareness can foster environmental stewardship. Supporting research and development of green technologies and incentivizing businesses in sustainable sectors drive economic growth while reducing environmental impact. Prioritizing sustainable development will create a prosperous, inclusive and environmentally sustainable future for India, aligning with global sustainability goals.

Defining Sustainable Development

Sustainable development aims to meet present needs without compromising future generations. It balances economic, social and environmental aspects—emphasizing environmental conservation, social equity, economic prosperity and inter-generational equity. To achieve sustainability, these principles must be integrated into areas like urban planning, energy production, transportation, agriculture and industry—ensuring a harmonious and equitable society while preserving natural resources and ecosystems.

The UN Sustainable Development Goals (SDGs), adopted in 2015, are a set of 17 global goals aimed at achieving a sustainable and equitable world by 2030. They encompass a range of areas including poverty eradication, education, gender equality, clean energy, climate action, sustainable cities and responsible consumption. The SDGs address social, economic and environmental aspects—emphasizing the need for collaboration among governments, businesses, civil society and individuals. Achieving the SDGs requires transformative action, partnerships, innovation and collective commitment. They provide specific targets and indicators to ensure accountability and offer a shared vision for a future that promotes sustainability and inclusivity for all.

The Present State of Sustainable Development in India and the Challenges before it

Sustainable development is of great importance in India due to the country's environmental challenges which include climate change, deforestation, water scarcity, pollution and land degradation. These challenges can have severe consequences for agriculture, public health and socio-economic well-being. By adopting sustainable practices, India can address these issues, promote a green economy and enhance resilience in the face of environmental changes.

India faces several challenges in achieving sustainable development. The country's large and growing population puts strain on natural resources, while rapid industrialization leads to increased pollution and resource depletion. Balancing industrial growth with environmental protection is essential. Sustainable agriculture and food security are also complex challenges. Transitioning to sustainable energy sources and managing waste efficiently are both crucial for environmental preservation. Furthermore, addressing poverty, climate change, water management, urban sustainability and the transition to a circular economy requires coordinated efforts from various stakeholders. Despite progress, these challenges require continued attention and action to achieve sustainable development in India.

Measures to overcome these challenges

To promote sustainable development in India, several key measures can be implemented. These include prioritizing environmental conservation and resource management, adopting renewable-energy sources, supporting sustainable agriculture and food security, implementing effective waste management and recycling practices, focusing on sustainable urbanization, promoting education and awareness on sustainability, fostering public–private partnerships, implementing policy reforms, directing investments towards sustainable projects and enhancing capacity building. By adopting these measures and taking a holistic approach to sustainable development, India can achieve economic growth, social progress and environmental stewardship for present and future generations. These efforts are essential to achieving national and international sustainable development goals.

10 Strategies by which India can ensure Sustainable Development

1. **Strengthen Policy Framework:** India should develop comprehensive policies that integrate sustainability principles across sectors. This involves aligning economic, social and environmental policies to promote sustainable practices. The government can establish regulatory frameworks, incentives and standards that encourage sustainable development and responsible business practices.

2. **Promote Renewable-Energy Transition:** India should accelerate the adoption of renewable-energy sources and

invest in related infrastructure. This includes expanding the use of solar, wind, hydro and other renewable-energy technologies to reduce reliance on fossil fuels. The government can provide incentives and support for renewable-energy projects, facilitate grid integration and promote research and development in clean-energy technologies.

3. **Foster Sustainable Agriculture:** India should promote sustainable agriculture practices. This includes encouraging organic farming—which reduces the use of chemical fertilizers and pesticides and also promotes soil health and biodiversity. Efficient water-management techniques such as drip irrigation and precision farming can minimize water usage. Agroforestry—which combines trees with agricultural crops—can enhance soil fertility, carbon sequestration and biodiversity.

4. **Improve Water-Resource Management:** India should implement efficient irrigation practices and policies for rainwater harvesting. This involves promoting water-efficient irrigation methods such as drip irrigation and sprinkler systems to minimize water wastage in agriculture. In addition to this, rainwater harvesting systems can be encouraged to capture and store rainwater for various purposes; this reduces the reliance on groundwater and mitigates water scarcity.

5. **Enhance Biodiversity Conservation:** India should prioritize the protection and conservation of biodiversity. This can be achieved by establishing protected areas, national parks and wildlife sanctuaries to safeguard ecosystems and endangered species. Promoting sustainable tourism practices that respect and preserve biodiversity can also contribute to conservation efforts.

6. **Strengthen Waste Management and Recycling:** India should focus on minimizing waste generation, promoting recycling and enforcing strict waste-disposal regulations. Implementing

effective waste-management systems—such as waste segregation, recycling facilities and proper disposal methods— can reduce environmental pollution and promote a circular economy.

7. **Promote Sustainable Transport:** India can invest in sustainable transportation options to reduce carbon emissions and congestion. This includes expanding public transportation networks, promoting the use of electric vehicles and improving infrastructure for non-motorized transport like cycling and walking. Encouraging the adoption of eco-friendly transportation options can help reduce air pollution and promote healthier and more sustainable cities.

8. **Encourage Green Building Practices:** India should promote energy-efficient and sustainable building practices. This involves raising awareness about the benefits of green buildings and providing incentives for their construction and renovation. Implementing energy-saving measures, using eco-friendly materials and adopting green building certifications can contribute to resource efficiency, reduced carbon footprint and improved indoor air quality.

9. **Focus on Public Awareness and Education:** India should conduct awareness campaigns to educate the public about sustainability and integrate it into education curricula at all levels. Engaging communities through workshops and initiatives can promote sustainable practices at the grassroots level.

10. **Support Research, Innovation and CSR:** India should invest in research and innovation for sustainable technologies while encouraging businesses to adopt sustainability through CSR initiatives. In addition to this, promoting international cooperation can enhance India's capacity for sustainable development and contribute to global sustainability efforts.

These steps require collective efforts from the government, businesses, civil society and individuals. By implementing these measures, India can make significant progress towards sustainable development—ensuring a prosperous, equitable and environmentally sustainable future.

Conclusion

Promoting sustainable development is vital for India's journey towards a developed-nation status by 2050. It fosters economic growth, resource efficiency, resilience, social equity, environmental preservation, sustainable urbanization and global leadership. By implementing sustainable practices in agriculture, industry and energy sectors, India can mitigate climate change, conserve natural resources and ensure environmental sustainability. This requires policy reforms, investments, innovation and collaborations, aligning development strategies with sustainability principles.

Overcoming challenges such as population pressure, industrial growth and energy transition requires a multi-faceted approach that includes policy frameworks, technology adoption, public awareness and international cooperation. By embracing sustainable development, India can create a green economy, protect its ecosystems and improve the quality of life for its citizens. Sustainable development is not only a responsibility towards future generations but also an opportunity to build India as a resilient, inclusive and prosperous nation by 2050.

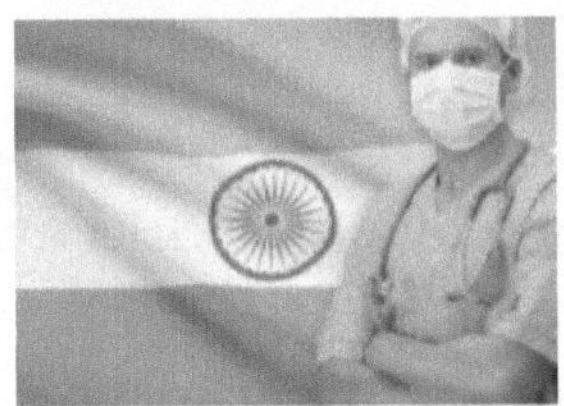

Strengthen Healthcare Systems

Introduction

Strengthening healthcare systems in India is vital for the country's development. It involves efforts like improving infrastructure, workforce, access, preventive care, financing, information systems, collaborations and regulations. Prioritizing healthcare can enhance the accessibility, quality, affordability and effectiveness of services, leading to improved well-being and health outcomes. A robust healthcare system is crucial for India's overall progress and prosperity.

A strong healthcare system in India has multiple benefits: it drives economic growth by ensuring a healthy workforce and reduces healthcare disparities through equitable access to services. It also plays a critical role in disease prevention and management, containing outbreaks and reducing disease burden. Healthcare also provides financial protection, promoting stability for families. Furthermore, investing in healthcare infrastructure and innovation fosters advancements, contributing to the growth of the healthcare sector. Overall, strengthening healthcare systems in India is essential for the nation's development—leading to a healthier, more prosperous and equitable society on the global stage.

Defining Healthcare Systems and efforts of present Government

Healthcare systems are organized networks that provide medical and health services to a population. They aim to promote, protect and restore health—encompassing healthcare facilities, professionals, equipment, insurance and policies. The main goal is to offer timely, appropriate and affordable healthcare services—addressing public health challenges and ensuring equitable access to medical care for all individuals. Healthcare systems may vary between countries in their structure, financing and public–private involvement. An effective healthcare system is crucial for improving overall health and well-being.

The Government of India has undertaken several initiatives to strengthen healthcare systems and services. The key efforts include the Ayushman Bharat–Pradhan Mantri Jan Arogya Yojana (PM-JAY) health insurance scheme, the National Health Mission (NHM) for rural healthcare and the Pradhan Mantri Swasthya Suraksha Yojana (PMSSY) to develop tertiary healthcare infrastructure. The National Medical Commission (NMC) Act, 2019, aims to reform medical education, while digital health initiatives like the National Digital Health Mission (NDHM) streamline healthcare data and access. Emphasis is placed on strengthening primary healthcare, responding to the COVID-19 pandemic and developing healthcare infrastructure nationwide. These efforts aim to expand coverage, improve infrastructure, enhance the healthcare workforce and leverage technology for better healthcare delivery.

The Present State of Healthcare Systems in India and the Challenges before it

The healthcare systems in India face a combination of achievements and challenges. Challenges include disparities in access, inadequate infrastructure, workforce shortages, affordability issues, varying quality of care, gaps in preventive care and public health, health information system integration, social determinants of health and the need for regulatory framework improvement. India can strengthen its healthcare system and improve healthcare delivery for the entire population by providing accessible, affordable and quality healthcare.

Measures to overcome these challenges

To strengthen healthcare systems, India can take measures such as increasing healthcare investments, expanding coverage through health insurance schemes, addressing workforce shortages, improving infrastructure, implementing effective policies, leveraging technology and innovation and fostering collaborations between stakeholders. These measures will help address challenges and improve healthcare access and quality for all citizens.

10 Strategies by which India can strengthen the Healthcare Systems

1. **Increase healthcare spending:** Allocate more funds to upgrade healthcare infrastructure, acquire advanced medical equipment and ensure access to essential medicines and vaccines. Adequate funding helps improve healthcare resources and services, leading to better health outcomes.

2. **Enhance primary healthcare:** Strengthen early detection, health promotion and preventive care by establishing more primary healthcare centres and building a skilled healthcare workforce. Primary healthcare plays a crucial role in disease prevention and reduces the burden on higher-level healthcare facilities.

3. **Develop a robust healthcare workforce:** Invest in the training and continuous development of healthcare professionals to

ensure competent and quality care. Skilled and compassionate healthcare workers are essential for delivering effective medical services.

4. **Emphasize preventive care:** Implement immunization programs and health education campaigns to reduce the incidence of preventable diseases. Preventive care helps promote overall population health and reduces the need for costly treatments.

5. **Implement health insurance schemes:** Expand health insurance coverage to provide financial protection for healthcare services, especially for vulnerable populations. Health insurance ensures equitable access to medical treatments and reduces out-of-pocket expenses.

6. **Strengthen rural healthcare:** Address healthcare access challenges in rural areas through strategies like telemedicine networks, mobile healthcare units and incentives for healthcare professionals to work in rural regions. These initiatives bridge the gap between urban and rural healthcare services.

7. **Promote innovation and technology:** Embrace healthcare technologies like telemedicine, electronic health records (EHRs) and digital health solutions to improve healthcare delivery, patient outcomes and accessibility. Technology can enhance efficiency and cost-effectiveness.

8. **Foster public–private partnerships:** Collaborate with private healthcare providers to enhance service delivery and address infrastructure gaps. Public–private partnerships leverage expertise and resources to improve healthcare quality and expand services.

9. **Strengthen health information systems and address social determinants of health:** Develop comprehensive health information systems for data collection and analysis, aiding evidence-based decision-making and resource allocation.

Simultaneously, address social determinants of health—such as poverty and education—to improve overall healthcare access and outcomes.

10. **Promote research and development and strengthen regulatory frameworks:** Encourage scientific research, indigenous drug discovery and medical advancements to meet specific healthcare needs. Strong regulatory frameworks ensure quality, safety and ethical standards in the healthcare sector, protecting patient rights and fostering public trust.

Conclusion

In conclusion, strengthening healthcare systems is crucial for India's development and its aspirations to become a developed country by 2050. By prioritizing healthcare, India can improve access to quality healthcare, enhance public health infrastructure and focus on preventive measures. Overcoming healthcare challenges requires policy reforms, infrastructure development, human resource development and innovative solutions. A robust healthcare system not only improves healthier outcomes but also reduces healthcare costs, enhances productivity and promotes socio-economic well-being. It is essential for the government, stakeholders and society to work together in prioritizing healthcare, implementing necessary measures and ensuring the availability of accessible and quality healthcare services. By doing so, India can build a healthier, more prosperous nation on its path to development.

Foster Good Governance

Introduction

Good governance is crucial for India's development, enabling effective decision-making, public service delivery and resource allocation. It promotes transparency, accountability and efficiency—reducing corruption and ensuring proper use of public funds. The key elements include economic growth, institutional strengthening, transparency, citizen participation, rule of law and social development. Challenges like corruption and lack of citizen involvement persist, but legal reforms, citizen engagement, capacity building and technological innovations can address them. Good governance builds public trust, promotes economic growth and fosters sustainable development for India's future.

Defining Good Governance

Good governance involves efficient and accountable resource management, decision-making and public services. It includes principles like transparency, rule of law, equity and participation. In India, fostering good governance is vital for progress and development. This entails implementing effective legal frameworks, combating corruption and promoting fair practices in public administration. In the context of India, fostering good governance is essential for the country's progress and development. It involves implementing effective legal and regulatory frameworks that promote transparency and accountability. By enacting and enforcing anti-corruption laws and protecting whistle-blowers, India can combat corruption and promote fair practices in public administration.

Citizen engagement and participation are crucial for good governance, involving public consultations and participatory budgeting to align policies with people's needs. Efficient service delivery is essential, achieved through streamlined processes and technology-driven solutions, improving transparency and public trust. Fostering good governance promotes economic growth, attracting investment and creating an environment conducive to development. To achieve India's vision of becoming a developed nation by 2050, addressing challenges like corruption and bureaucratic inefficiencies through legal reforms and citizen involvement is vital. Embracing good governance principles establishes a strong foundation for sustainable progress and prosperity for all citizens.

The Present State of Governance in India and the Challenges before it

The present state of good governance in India reflects both progress and challenges. On one hand, the government has made commendable efforts in promoting digital transformation, implementing anti-corruption measures, fostering financial inclusion and simplifying administrative procedures. These initiatives have led to increased transparency, efficiency and accessibility of public services, as well as enhanced financial transparency and reduced leakages in welfare schemes. Furthermore, citizen participation has been encouraged through platforms like MyGov and participatory budgeting, allowing citizens to have a say in decision-making processes.

However, challenges persist in the form of corruption, bureaucratic red tape, limited transparency in certain sectors, judicial delays and the need for greater citizen participation. Corruption remains a significant hindrance to good governance, eroding transparency and accountability in government institutions. The bureaucratic red tape creates administrative inefficiencies, making it cumbersome for citizens to access government services. Limited transparency in some sectors leads to a lack of public trust in the functioning of government institutions. Judicial delays pose a significant challenge in delivering timely justice to citizens.

Measures to overcome these Challenges

To enhance good governance in India, targeted reforms are proposed. These include enforcing strict anti-corruption laws and establishing independent anti-corruption agencies, streamlining administrative procedures, emphasizing transparency through proactive information disclosure and digitization, implementing judicial reforms to address case backlogs, promoting citizen participation in decision-making, providing capacity building for government officials, fostering ethical leadership and utilizing technology for e-governance and open data initiatives. By implementing these measures, India can strengthen good governance, leading to sustainable development and improved well-being for all citizens.

10 Strategies by which India can foster Good Governance

To ensure that India becomes a developed country by 2050, fostering good governance is of paramount importance. Implementing the following ten steps can contribute significantly to achieving this goal:

1. **Strengthening Legal and Regulatory Frameworks:** India can foster good governance by enacting and enforcing strong laws and regulations that promote transparency, accountability and the rule of law. This includes implementing anti-corruption legislation, providing whistle-blower protection and ensuring

the independence of regulatory bodies to oversee different sectors effectively.

2. **Promoting Citizen Participation:** Active citizen engagement is vital for good governance. India can achieve this by encouraging public consultations on policy decisions, implementing participatory budgeting to involve citizens in financial decision-making and establishing mechanisms for feedback and input from the public.

3. **Enhancing Transparency and Access to Information:** Transparency is a key pillar of good governance. India can promote transparency by proactively disclosing information, digitizing records and creating online portals for easy access to government data and information.

4. **Strengthening Anti-Corruption Measures:** To combat corruption effectively, India must implement comprehensive anti-corruption measures. This includes establishing independent anti-corruption agencies, promoting integrity in public administration and ensuring swift and impartial prosecution of corrupt officials.

5. **Improving Service Delivery:** Streamlining administrative processes and reducing bureaucratic red tape will lead to more efficient and effective service delivery. Digitizing service delivery can further enhance accessibility and responsiveness to citizen needs.

6. **Empowering Local Governments:** Devolving power, resources and decision-making authority to local governments empowers citizens to actively participate in decision-making and local development. This strengthens democracy and ensures governance that is responsive to local needs.

7. **Promoting Ethical Leadership and Accountability:** Fostering a culture of ethics and accountability among public officials

is crucial. India can achieve this through leadership-training programs, implementing codes of conduct and enforcing strict disciplinary measures for misconduct.

8. **Harnessing Technology:** Investing in digital infrastructure and promoting open data initiatives can significantly improve governance. Leveraging technology can lead to efficient service delivery, better data management and increased citizen engagement.

9. **Strengthening the Judicial System:** India can address challenges faced by the judiciary by reducing case backlogs, improving infrastructure and adopting technology-driven solutions for case management. This ensures timely and fair dispensation of justice.

10. **Building Capacities and Ensuring Continuous Learning:** Providing training and capacity-building programs for public officials is essential. This enhances their skills, knowledge and understanding of governance principles, leading to more effective implementation of policies and programs.

By undertaking these ten steps, India can create a governance framework that fosters transparency, accountability and efficiency. This will contribute to sustainable development, economic growth and improved well-being for its citizens. It is essential to implement these measures holistically and with a commitment to realize the vision of a developed India by 2050.

Conclusion

Fostering good governance is a transformative journey for India, with the potential to make it a developed country by 2050. This involves various aspects such as economic prosperity, reduced corruption, technological advancement, democratic values and sustainable development. To achieve this vision, continuous efforts, commitment from leaders and citizen participation are essential. Addressing challenges, implementing reforms and upholding transparency and accountability are crucial. By doing so, India can unlock its true potential and become a prosperous and influential nation globally.

Boost Manufacturing and Industry

Introduction

The manufacturing and industry sector's development is crucial for India's progress, offering opportunities for job creation, economic growth and technological advancements. However, challenges like complex regulations, inadequate infrastructure and skill gaps need to be addressed. Policy reforms, infrastructure investments and skill-enhancement programs are necessary to overcome these challenges. International collaborations can also boost the sector by facilitating technology transfer and foreign direct investment. By effectively addressing these issues, India can establish a competitive manufacturing sector, contributing to its vision of becoming a developed country.

Defining Manufacturing and Industry

Manufacturing refers to the process of transforming raw materials or components into finished goods through various production processes. It involves the use of machines, tools and labour to create products that are ready for consumption or use. Industry, on the other hand, is a broader term that encompasses various sectors involved in the production, processing or extraction of goods and services. It includes manufacturing as well as other sectors such as agriculture, mining, construction and services.

In the context of India's development, boosting manufacturing and industry is essential for achieving economic growth, creating jobs and advancing technological capabilities. By investing in supportive policies, infrastructure and innovation, India can enhance its manufacturing and industrial sectors, reduce unemployment, improve competitiveness and reduce reliance on imports. Emphasizing skill development, improving infrastructure and creating a conducive environment for investment and entrepreneurship will be crucial in harnessing the full potential of manufacturing and industry to drive India's progress towards becoming a developed nation by 2050.

The Present State of Indian Manufacturing & Industry and the Challenges before it

The Indian government has undertaken various initiatives and reforms to boost manufacturing and industry in the country. Some of the key measures include the 'Make in India' Initiative, GST implementation, National Manufacturing Policy and the development of industrial corridors. Skill-development programs, ease-of-doing-business reforms and production-linked incentive schemes have also been introduced to support the manufacturing sector. Infrastructure development, research and development initiatives and sector-specific reforms further enhance India's manufacturing capabilities and global competitiveness. These efforts aim to accelerate economic growth, create jobs and establish India as a leading global manufacturing hub.

The current state of boosting manufacturing and industry in India has shown progress, but there are significant challenges that still need to be addressed. These challenges include infrastructure deficiencies, complex regulatory procedures, shortages of skilled workforce, limited access to finance for SMEs and the need for technology adoption and innovation in the manufacturing sector. Overcoming these obstacles will be crucial to fully harness the potential of manufacturing and industry in India and achieve sustainable growth and development.

Measures to overcome these Challenges

To boost manufacturing and industry in India, several measures can be implemented including policy reforms, infrastructure development, skill enhancement, improved access to finance, technology adoption, cluster development, export promotion, support for SMEs, industry–academia collaboration and sustainable manufacturing practices. By implementing these strategies, India can overcome challenges and foster a thriving manufacturing sector—contributing to economic growth, job creation, technological advancements and progress towards becoming a developed nation.

10 Strategies by which India can boost Manufacturing & Industry

1. **Simplify Regulatory Frameworks:** India should focus on streamlining and simplifying its regulatory processes. Reducing bureaucratic red tape and creating a business-friendly environment will encourage investment and ease the burden on businesses. This includes rationalizing licenses, permits and approvals required for setting up and operating businesses.

2. **Improve Ease-of-Doing-Business:** Implementing reforms to enhance India's ranking in the Ease–of-Doing-Business index is crucial. This involves digitizing processes, reducing the time and cost of starting a business and expediting approvals and clearances. Simplifying procedures and reducing administrative burdens will encourage entrepreneurship and promote a vibrant manufacturing and industry sector.

3. **Enhance Infrastructure Development:** Investment in the development of robust infrastructure is essential for the growth of manufacturing and industry. This includes transportation networks, logistics hubs, industrial parks and reliable power supply. The development of infrastructure facilitates smooth operations, reduces costs and enhances the competitiveness of manufacturing industries. Well-connected transportation

networks and modern industrial parks attract investment and support efficient production and distribution.

4. **Promote Skill Development:** To meet the demands of modern manufacturing techniques and technologies, India needs a skilled and trained workforce. Focusing on skill-development programs that align with industry requirements is crucial. Enhancing vocational training, apprenticeship programs and collaboration between educational institutions and industries can ensure a skilled workforce that meets the demands of the manufacturing sector. By equipping individuals with industry-relevant skills, the sector can thrive and grow.

5. **Encourage Research and Development:** Fostering innovation and research and development (R&D) in the manufacturing sector is vital for staying competitive. This can be achieved by providing incentives for R&D activities, supporting technology incubators and innovation clusters and encouraging collaboration between industry and academia. Investing in R&D leads to technological advancements, increased productivity and improved competitiveness.

6. **Attract Foreign Direct Investment (FDI):** Creating an attractive investment climate to encourage foreign companies to invest in India's manufacturing sector is essential. Implementing FDI-friendly policies, offering incentives and simplifying procedures for setting up and operating businesses will attract more foreign direct investment. FDI brings in capital, technology and expertise—contributing to the growth of the manufacturing sector.

7. **Facilitate Access to Finance:** Improving access to affordable finance for manufacturing enterprises, particularly for small and medium-sized enterprises (SMEs), is crucial for their growth. Measures such as easing collateral requirements, providing credit guarantee schemes and promoting alternative

financing options can support the growth of the sector. Access to finance enables businesses to invest in machinery, technology and expansion.

8. **Foster Industry–Academia Collaboration:** Strengthening collaboration between industries and academic institutions can bridge the gap between theoretical knowledge and practical industry requirements. Promoting joint research projects, internships and industry visits enhances industry-relevant skills among students. Collaboration ensures that the workforce is equipped with the latest knowledge and skills needed in the manufacturing sector.

9. **Support Cluster Development:** Promoting the development of manufacturing clusters that bring together related industries, suppliers and support services is beneficial. Clusters facilitate economies of scale, knowledge sharing and collaboration—leading to enhanced competitiveness. The development of clusters helps create a conducive ecosystem where businesses can thrive and benefit from shared resources and expertise.

10. **Promote Export-Oriented Manufacturing:** Focusing on sectors with export potential and providing necessary support to boost exports is crucial. This includes improving logistics, simplifying export procedures and providing incentives for export-oriented manufacturing. Increasing exports contributes to economic growth, job creation and the diversification of markets.

By implementing these strategies, India can overcome challenges and foster a thriving manufacturing and industry sector, contributing to sustainable economic growth, job creation, technological advancements and progress towards becoming a developed nation. Continued efforts and collaboration between the government, industry stakeholders and academia are vital to achieving these goals.

Conclusion

Boosting manufacturing and industry plays a crucial role in India's path to becoming a developed country by 2050. By focusing on these sectors, India can achieve significant economic growth, create employment opportunities, foster technological advancements, improve infrastructure, enhance export competitiveness and promote sustainable development. The ten steps outlined such as simplifying regulations, improving infrastructure, promoting skill development, fostering innovation and encouraging exports are vital in realizing this vision. Collaboration between the government, private sector, academia and citizens is crucial in driving these sectors forward. By harnessing the potential of manufacturing and industry, India can establish a self-sufficient and thriving economy, ensuring a better quality of life for its citizens and achieving its goal of becoming a developed nation by 2050.

Promote Financial Inclusion

Introduction

Financial inclusion is vital for India's development, providing access to financial services for individuals and businesses. However, challenges like low financial literacy, inadequate infrastructure and the digital divide hinder progress. Strategies such as financial literacy programs, mobile banking and simplified account opening can address these issues. Incentivizing institutions and promoting public–private collaborations can further boost inclusion.

The benefits are significant including economic growth, reduced reliance on the informal economy, enhanced social welfare, women empowerment and poverty reduction. To achieve widespread financial inclusion, India needs to expand access, simplify procedures, provide financial literacy, tailor products and implement regulatory reforms. By addressing challenges and implementing effective strategies, India can foster inclusive growth, empower women and create a stable and prosperous society—aligning with its vision of becoming a developed country by 2050.

Defining Financial Inclusion

Financial inclusion aims to provide accessible and affordable financial services to all segments of society, including those traditionally excluded. It empowers individuals and communities, reduces poverty, promotes economic growth and fosters stability. This involves not only access to financial services but also financial education and leveraging digital technologies. The goal is to create a more inclusive and equitable society where everyone has equal opportunities for economic participation and improved quality of life.

The Present State of Financial Inclusion and the Challenges before it

The Indian government has undertaken several initiatives to promote financial inclusion and expand access to financial services, such as the Pradhan Mantri Jan Dhan Yojana (PMJDY), Direct Benefit Transfer (DBT) and promoting digital payments. Small finance banks and payment banks have played a role in serving underserved segments. The Financial Inclusion Index (FII) helps track progress and implements targeted interventions. Jan Suraksha Schemes provide affordable financial protection while financial literacy initiatives aim to empower individuals.

These efforts have made significant strides in promoting financial inclusion, but challenges like reaching remote areas, low financial literacy, informal financial channels and gender disparity remain.

Measures to overcome these Challenges

To overcome these challenges, the measures include expanding digital and physical infrastructure, enhancing financial literacy programs, strengthening regulations to promote inclusive practices, tailoring financial products to meet specific needs and promoting the financial inclusion of women. A multi-faceted approach involving government, financial institutions and other stakeholders is essential for achieving sustainable and inclusive financial inclusion in India.

10 Strategies by which India can promote Financial Inclusion

1. **Expand Access to Basic Banking Services:** Financial inclusion begins with ensuring that basic banking services are available to all segments of the population. To achieve this, India should establish banking outlets—especially in rural and underserved areas—and open more bank branches, making financial services easily accessible to people.

2. **Enhance Digital Financial Infrastructure:** To promote financial inclusion, India needs a robust digital financial infrastructure. This requires investments in expanding internet connectivity in rural areas and improving mobile network coverage. A strong digital infrastructure will enable more people to access digital financial services and engage in cashless transactions. Promoting digital payment systems like Unified Payments Interface (UPI) and encouraging the use of mobile wallets will facilitate convenient and secure digital transactions, particularly through smartphones, making them accessible to a large portion of the population.

3. **Promote Financial Literacy and Education:** Financial literacy is crucial for empowering individuals to make informed financial decisions and effectively use financial services. Comprehensive programs should educate people about basic financial concepts, responsible behaviour, saving, budgeting and digital financial services. The focus should extend to both urban and rural areas, with particular attention given to underprivileged and marginalized communities. By providing financial education, individuals can enhance their financial well-being by understanding and utilizing financial products and services effectively.

4. **Strengthen Consumer Protection:** Consumer protection is essential for instilling trust in the formal financial system. Strong regulations ensure fair treatment and protection from

fraud. Transparent pricing, terms and conditions empower customers to make informed choices. Efficient grievance redressal mechanisms address complaints promptly, ensuring satisfactory resolutions for customers.

5. **Encourage Microfinance and Small-Ticket Loans:** Microfinance institutions (MFIs) have been instrumental in serving underserved populations, particularly in rural areas, by providing financial services. Supporting and enabling the growth of MFIs will help them offer small-ticket loans to those who lack access to traditional banking. To mitigate risks, credit guarantee schemes can be introduced, providing a safety net for lenders and encouraging them to extend credit to underserved communities.

6. **Foster Collaboration between Banks and Fintech Companies:** Collaboration between traditional banks and fintech companies can lead to innovation and broader financial service accessibility. Fintech companies use technology to offer innovative solutions, while banks provide an extensive customer base and resources. Regulatory sandboxes enable experimentation while ensuring compliance and consumer protection.

7. **Leverage Aadhaar and Digital ID:** The Aadhaar biometric identification system is instrumental in promoting financial inclusion. Aadhaar-based customer on-boarding simplifies the account opening process, thus eliminating paperwork. Aadhaar-based e-KYC enables paperless verification, making it easier, especially for those in remote areas, to open bank accounts and access financial services.

8. **Promote Agents and Business Correspondents:** In areas where physical bank branches are impractical, using agents and business correspondents can extend financial services to underserved and remote regions. Incentivizing these agents

promotes outreach and accessibility to unbanked and under-banked populations.

9. **Support the Financial Inclusion of Women:** Gender-specific challenges hinder the financial inclusion of women and decrease their economic opportunities. Targeted programs including gender-specific financial products, such as savings accounts and loans, can address these issues. Tailored financial literacy programs empower women to make informed decisions and participate in economic activities.

10. **Monitor and Evaluate Progress:** A comprehensive monitoring and evaluation framework is crucial for assessing the impact of financial inclusion initiatives. Regular data analysis helps identify gaps, measure progress and understand the effectiveness of strategies. Data-driven decisions enable policymakers and stakeholders to adjust approaches and work towards sustained financial inclusion.

By undertaking these ten steps, India can create a more inclusive financial ecosystem, improve access to financial services and foster economic growth for all segments of society. Financial inclusion is not only a means to economic growth but also a way to foster social development, reduce poverty and create a more equitable society. By 2050, India can realize its vision of becoming a developed nation, where every citizen has access to the financial tools and services necessary for a prosperous future.

Conclusion

Promoting financial inclusion is crucial for India's development as a developed nation by 2050. Collaboration among various stakeholders—including the government, financial institutions, technology companies and civil society organizations—is key to achieving this goal. Strategies like expanding access to banking services, enhancing digital infrastructure and promoting financial literacy and consumer protection are vital. Encouraging microfinance, fostering bank-fintech collaboration, leveraging digital identification and supporting the financial inclusion of women are essential steps. Successful financial inclusion will lead to inclusive economic growth, poverty reduction, reduced inequality, enhanced financial resilience and empowerment. Continued collaboration and monitoring progress are necessary for India's vision of a prosperous and equitable nation with equal access to financial services for all citizens. Financial inclusion plays a pivotal role in ensuring India's sustainable and inclusive development towards becoming a developed country by 2050.

Harness Renewable Energy

Introduction

Renewable energy plays a vital role in India's development as it addresses energy security, electricity demand and environmental sustainability. It reduces the dependence on imported fossil fuels, enhances energy security and provides scalable and sustainable solutions for increasing electricity needs. Transitioning to renewables promotes environmental sustainability, reduces carbon emissions and improves air quality, aligning with global climate goals. Furthermore, the renewable energy sector drives economic growth, creates job opportunities, fosters innovation and contributes to rural development. Prioritizing renewables supports a sustainable and inclusive development path for India while contributing to global climate efforts.

Defining Renewable Energy

Renewable energy refers to energy derived from natural sources such as sunlight, wind, water and biomass. It plays a vital role in India's development as it offers multiple benefits. By harnessing renewable energy, India can achieve energy security by reducing its dependence on imported fossil fuels. It also provides a sustainable solution to meet the country's growing electricity demand, ensuring a stable and reliable energy supply. One of the significant advantages of renewable energy is its contribution to environmental sustainability. Unlike fossil fuels, renewable-energy sources do not produce greenhouse gas emissions, which are a major contributor to climate change. Transitioning to renewables helps reduce carbon emissions, improve air quality and align with global efforts to combat climate change.

The renewable-energy sector serves as a significant catalyst for economic growth and job creation. Investing in renewable-energy projects stimulates economic activity and attracts private investments, leading to employment opportunities in various stages: from manufacturing to installation and maintenance. By prioritizing the integration of renewable energy into its energy mix, India can achieve sustainable and inclusive development. This approach ensures energy security, protects the environment and contributes to poverty alleviation and rural development. Embracing renewable energy is a crucial step for India's path towards becoming a developed nation, while also aligning with global efforts to create a more sustainable and environmentally friendly future.

The Present State of Renewable Energy and the Challenges before it

The present state of renewable energy in India shows commendable progress, thanks to the government's proactive initiatives and policies driving growth. The country has placed significant emphasis on solar and wind power and co-founded the International Solar Alliance, contributing to India's energy transition and positively influencing global renewable-energy adoption. The key achievement includes establishing Green Energy Corridors, facilitating the seamless integration of renewable energy into the grid. By modernizing grid infrastructure and implementing advanced management systems, India effectively manages the variable nature of solar and wind power, ensuring a stable and reliable energy supply.

Embracing renewable-energy technologies in India promises improved efficiency, cost reduction and attracts both domestic and international investments, thereby fostering economic growth and job creation. India's commitment to combating climate change and ensuring environmental sustainability is demonstrated through the widespread adoption of renewable energy. Moreover, extending renewable energy to rural areas empowers local communities and fosters inclusive growth. India's participation in international efforts, such as the International Solar Alliance, positions it as a global leader in the transition to clean energy.

Ultimately, prioritizing renewable energy is crucial for India's sustainable development and sets an inspiring example for the world. By aiming for a thriving, prosperous and environmentally conscious nation by 2050, India underscores the importance of renewable energy as a strategic move towards becoming a developed country. However, while India's progress is commendable, there are still challenges ahead such as grid integration, securing affordable financing and addressing land acquisition for large-scale projects. Overcoming these challenges will be essential to ensuring continued growth and success in India's renewable-energy journey.

Measures to Overcome the Challenges

Measures to overcome the challenges and harness renewable energy in India include investing in grid modernization and smart grid technologies; exploring innovative financing mechanisms; implementing effective land management strategies; ensuring policy certainty; promoting capacity building and skill development; encouraging research and development; raising public awareness and participation; fostering public–private partnerships; streamlining approval processes and creating a supportive regulatory environment. By implementing these measures, India can effectively tap into its renewable-energy potential, advance its sustainable development goals and contribute to a greener and cleaner energy future. Continued commitment from all stakeholders is crucial in achieving India's renewable-energy targets and transitioning to a more sustainable energy system.

10 Strategies by which India can harness Renewable Energy

1. **Set Ambitious Renewable-Energy Targets:** India should establish ambitious and realistic targets for renewable-energy deployment, including specific goals for each renewable-energy sector. These targets can provide a clear roadmap and direction for the country's renewable-energy development.

2. **Enhance Policy and Regulatory Frameworks:** Continually review and update policies and regulations to provide a stable and favourable environment for renewable-energy investments. Streamline approval processes, offer transparent and predictable policies and provide incentives and subsidies to attract private-sector participation.

3. **Strengthen Grid Infrastructure:** Invest in upgrading the grid infrastructure to accommodate the increased penetration of renewable energy. Modernize transmission and distribution networks, implement advanced grid management systems and promote the adoption of energy storage technologies to ensure grid stability and seamless integration of renewable energy.

4. **Promote Research and Development:** Increase investments in research and development (R&D) for renewable-energy technologies. Encourage collaboration between research institutions, industry and government to develop innovative solutions, improve efficiency and reduce the cost of renewable-energy technologies.

5. **Facilitate Access to Finance:** Establish mechanisms to enhance access to affordable financing for renewable-energy

projects. This can include promoting green finance, creating dedicated funds, providing credit enhancements and facilitating partnerships between financial institutions and renewable-energy developers.

6. **Encourage Public–Private Partnerships:** Foster collaboration between the public and private sectors to accelerate renewable-energy deployment. Public–private partnerships can leverage the strengths of the sectors, share risks and rewards and drive investment and innovation in the renewable-energy sector.

7. **Promote Energy Efficiency:** Emphasize energy efficiency measures to complement renewable-energy deployment. Implement energy efficiency standards and labelling programs, promote energy-efficient appliances and buildings and raise awareness about the benefits of energy conservation.

8. **Skill Development and Capacity Building:** Establish training programs and initiatives to develop a skilled workforce for the renewable-energy sector. Focus on vocational training, capacity building and educational programs to enhance knowledge and skills in renewable-energy technologies, project management and maintenance.

9. **Encourage Decentralized Renewable-Energy Systems:** Promote the adoption of decentralized renewable-energy systems such as off-grid solar, mini-grids and rooftop solar installations. These systems can provide electricity to remote areas, enhance energy access and support rural development.

10. **International Cooperation and Knowledge Sharing:** Collaborate with international partners, organizations and forums to share best practices; learn from global experiences and access technology and financing support. Engaging in international cooperation can accelerate India's renewable-energy development and foster innovation.

By implementing these ten steps, India can create a conducive environment for harnessing renewable energy—promoting sustainable development, ensuring energy security and thus progressing towards becoming a developed nation.

Conclusion

In conclusion, India's journey towards becoming a developed country by 2050 hinges on harnessing renewable energy. Adopting renewable sources like solar, wind and hydropower offers numerous benefits—including sustainable economic growth, enhanced energy security, environmental preservation and inclusive development. By investing in renewables, India can meet its escalating energy demands, reduce dependence on imported fossil fuels and shield itself from external price fluctuations. Embracing renewable energy will lead to improved efficiency, lower costs and attract investments—fuelling economic growth and job creation. India's commitment to combating climate change through renewable adoption positions it as a global leader, while extending renewable energy to rural areas empowers local communities. Prioritizing renewable energy ensures India's sustainable development and sets an inspiring example for the world, aspiring to be a thriving, prosperous and environmentally conscious nation by 2050.

Improve Rural Development

Introduction

Improving rural development in India is essential due to its significant rural population and vast land area. Neglecting rural areas can cause regional disparities and hinder inclusive and sustainable development. Addressing challenges like education, healthcare and infrastructure can uplift living standards and create economic opportunities. Supporting agriculture and rural entrepreneurship contributes to economic growth. Rural development can also reduce rural–urban migration and promote sustainable urbanization. Emphasizing environmental sustainability is crucial. Ultimately, prioritizing rural development leads to inclusive progress and prosperity for all citizens.

Defining Rural Development

Rural development refers to the process of improving the economic, social and environmental well-being of rural areas and their communities. It involves implementing various initiatives and strategies to address the unique challenges faced by rural regions, with the ultimate goal of achieving inclusive growth and sustainable progress.

Improving rural development is crucial for India's path to becoming a developed nation by 2050. It ensures inclusive growth, alleviates poverty and enhances human capital development. By boosting agricultural productivity and investing in rural areas, the government can achieve balanced regional development and promote sustainability. Strengthening rural–urban linkages, generating employment, fostering social cohesion and enhancing global competitiveness is vital for overall progress. By prioritizing rural infrastructure, education, healthcare and sustainable practices, India can create a prosperous and harmonious nation for all its citizens.

What has India done to ensure rural development in recent years?

In recent years, the Indian government has undertaken several initiatives to improve rural development. Some of the key programs and policies include:

1. **Pradhan Mantri Gram Sadak Yojana (PMGSY):** This program aims to provide all-weather road connectivity to rural areas, improving accessibility and connectivity for rural communities.

2. **Mahatma Gandhi National Rural Employment Guarantee Act (MGNREGA):** It guarantees 100 days of wage employment per year to rural households, providing income support and creating rural assets through various developmental activities.

3. **Deen Dayal Upadhyaya Grameen Kaushalya Yojana (DDU-GKY):** This scheme focuses on providing skill-development training to rural youth, enabling them to acquire employable skills and improve their livelihood opportunities.

4. **Pradhan Mantri Awas Yojana - Gramin (PMAY-G):** This program aims to provide affordable housing to rural households, improving their living conditions and promoting inclusive development.

5. **Saansad Adarsh Gram Yojana (SAGY):** This initiative encourages Members of Parliament (MPs) to adopt and develop model villages by providing them with funds for various developmental projects.

6. **Digital India:** This ambitious program aims to transform India into a digitally empowered society and knowledge economy by providing digital services and technology to rural areas.

7. **Swachh Bharat Mission (SBM):** The mission focuses on promoting sanitation and cleanliness in rural areas to improve public health and hygiene.

8. **Rashtriya Krishi Vikas Yojana (RKVY):** This program provides financial assistance to states for agricultural development, to enhance the agricultural productivity and income of farmers.

9. **Pradhan Mantri Fasal Bima Yojana (PMFBY):** This scheme provides crop insurance to farmers to mitigate the risks associated with crop failure due to natural calamities, pests and diseases.

10. **Kisan Credit Card (KCC) Scheme:** This initiative provides farmers with access to affordable credit and short-term loans for agricultural activities, helping them invest in farming and allied sectors.

These initiatives, along with other rural development projects and policies, are focused on improving rural infrastructure, promoting livelihood opportunities, enhancing agricultural productivity and empowering rural communities. They play a vital role in reducing poverty, bridging the rural–urban divide and fostering inclusive growth across the country. India's commitment to rural development is essential for achieving its long-term goal of becoming a developed nation by 2050.

The Present State of Rural Development and the Challenges before it

Improving rural development in India involves addressing challenges like poverty and income inequality, agricultural productivity, basic services and gender inequality. To overcome these challenges, the government should adopt an integrated approach, increase investments in rural infrastructure, promote financial inclusion, encourage technology adoption, strengthen institutions, emphasize skill development and entrepreneurship and focus on social inclusion and empowerment. Furthermore, research and development in agriculture and rural technologies can lead to sustainable development and inclusive growth, ensuring a balanced and prosperous India with active rural participation in the country's progress.

Improving rural development in India requires addressing challenges such as poverty and income disparities, agricultural productivity, basic services and infrastructure and gender inequality. This calls for targeted poverty alleviation programs, agricultural reforms, increased investment in infrastructure and promoting gender equality through awareness and skill training. A comprehensive and collaborative approach is essential to bring about meaningful and sustainable improvements in rural areas.

Measures to overcome the challenges before improving Rural Development

To overcome challenges in rural development, India should adopt an integrated approach, invest in rural infrastructure, expand financial inclusion, promote technology adoption, strengthen institutions, focus on skill development and entrepreneurship, prioritize social inclusion and empowerment and encourage research and development. By implementing these measures, India can achieve inclusive growth, reduce poverty and ensure sustainable development in rural areas, contributing to a balanced and prosperous nation.

To improve rural development in India and advance towards becoming a developed nation, the following ten strategies can be implemented:

1. **Comprehensive Rural Development Strategy:** Develop a holistic approach that addresses infrastructure, livelihoods, social welfare and sustainability needs in rural areas.

2. **Enhance Agricultural Productivity:** Promote modern farming practices, access to credit and technology adoption to increase agricultural output and improve farmers' incomes.

3. **Rural Infrastructure Development:** Invest in rural infrastructure like roads, electricity, water supply and sanitation to enhance connectivity and access to services.

4. **Skill Development and Entrepreneurship:** Provide targeted skill-training programs to cater to rural industries and encourage entrepreneurship to create employment opportunities.

5. **Access to Quality Education:** Improve educational facilities and promote digital learning initiatives in rural areas while focusing on trained teachers and girls' education.

6. **Healthcare Access:** Strengthen healthcare infrastructure with primary centres and mobile medical units to ensure accessible and affordable healthcare services.

7. **Financial Inclusion:** Expand banking services and microfinance options to increase financial access and availability of credit for rural entrepreneurs and farmers.

8. **Social-Welfare Programs:** Implement specific schemes to address poverty, nutrition and social disparities, thus providing social security, livelihood support and healthcare benefits to vulnerable populations.

9. **Environmental Conservation:** Promote sustainable practices, afforestation, watershed management and adoption of renewable energy to conserve resources and combat climate-change challenges.

10. **Community Participation and Empowerment:** Encourage community involvement, strengthen local governance and empower rural communities to participate in decision-making and take ownership of development initiatives.

Implementing these strategies with a long-term vision can lead to inclusive growth, poverty reduction, enhanced livelihood opportunities and sustainable rural development in India, ultimately contributing to the country's overall progress and prosperity.

Conclusion

In conclusion, rural development is integral to India's transformation into a developed nation by 2050. By investing in rural infrastructure, enhancing agricultural productivity and promoting education and skill development, India can empower its rural population and achieve inclusive growth. Bridging the rural–urban divide, ensuring financial inclusion and fostering sustainable practices will contribute to a balanced and equitable development path. As rural communities thrive, they will become hubs of innovation and economic growth. A holistic approach that embraces social, economic and environmental dimensions will lead India towards a future of prosperity and well-being for all its citizens. By committing to comprehensive rural development, India can harness the potential of its rural population and create a strong foundation for a developed and prosperous nation by 2050.

Strengthen Social-Welfare Programs

Introduction

India's development faces challenges due to its diverse and populous nature. Strengthening social-welfare programs is crucial to address these challenges and achieve inclusive growth. These programs play a significant role in supporting vulnerable communities and providing essential services, reducing poverty and inequality. Furthermore, they contribute to human capital development by ensuring access to education and healthcare. Social-welfare measures also foster social cohesion and unity by promoting inclusion and addressing disparities. By investing in and improving social-welfare programs, India can create a just and prosperous society—unlocking its human capital's potential and becoming a compassionate and progressive nation on the global stage.

Defining Social-Welfare Programs

Social-welfare programs are a set of government initiatives and policies designed to provide assistance and support to vulnerable and disadvantaged sections of society. These programs aim to address poverty, inequality and social exclusion by offering a safety net of essential services and financial aid. The range of services covered by social-welfare programs includes healthcare, education, food security, housing, unemployment benefits and social-security measures.

The primary objective of these programs is to uplift the living standards of the underprivileged and ensure their well-being. By offering access to education and skill development, social-welfare programs contribute to human capital development, creating a skilled and productive workforce. Moreover, these initiatives foster social cohesion by promoting inclusion and reducing discrimination, thereby creating a more equitable and stable society. Social-welfare programs are vital tools in addressing socio-economic challenges and building a developed nation where every citizen has equal opportunities and a dignified quality of life. By focusing on strengthening these programs, India can work towards achieving inclusive growth and reducing poverty, ultimately positioning itself as a compassionate and progressive nation on the global stage.

The Present State of Indian Social-Welfare Programs and the Challenges before them

Indian social-welfare programs have made significant progress in addressing various socio-economic challenges and improving the well-being of vulnerable populations. The present state of Indian Social-welfare programs reflects progress in various areas such as financial inclusion, healthcare, education, sanitation and food security. However, challenges persist in areas like sustaining active usage of bank accounts, improving healthcare infrastructure, addressing education quality and dropout rates, ensuring sustainable sanitation practices and preventing leakages and improving beneficiary identification.

Challenges before Indian Social-welfare programs include implementation inefficiencies, targeting and identification issues, limited access and awareness in rural areas, funding and resource constraints, governance and accountability issues, data management concerns and social and cultural barriers. Addressing these challenges and strengthening social-welfare programs is crucial for achieving inclusive and sustainable development, reducing poverty and fostering a more equitable society in India.

Measures to overcome these Challenges

The present state of social-welfare programs in India shows progress, but challenges remain. To enhance the impact and effectiveness of these initiatives, measures such as financial literacy campaigns, improving healthcare infrastructure, aligning skill-development programs with industry needs, leveraging technology for accurate targeting and strengthening accountability mechanisms are recommended. In addition to these, addressing gender disparities, improving administrative capacity and promoting transparency through public awareness campaigns and multi-stakeholder collaboration are also essential.

To strengthen social-welfare programs in India measures such as improving implementation mechanisms, accurate targeting, awareness campaigns, adequate funding, capacity building, transparent grievance redressal, public–private partnerships, monitoring and evaluation, gender mainstreaming, evidence-based policy changes, coordination and innovation can be undertaken. By implementing these steps, India can enhance the effectiveness of social-welfare programs, leading to inclusive and sustainable development, poverty reduction and improved well-being for all citizens.

10 Strategies by which India can strengthen Social-Welfare Programs

1. **Universal Basic Income (UBI):** Implementing a Universal Basic Income can provide financial security to all citizens, especially those in need. By providing a guaranteed minimum income, UBI can alleviate poverty and reduce income disparities. It offers a safety net during economic downturns and ensures that every citizen has access to a basic standard of living.

2. **Targeted Social Assistance:** Refining targeting mechanisms is essential to ensure that social-welfare benefits reach those who need them the most. By leveraging technology and data analytics, the government can accurately identify vulnerable populations and provide them with the necessary support and assistance.

3. **Holistic Healthcare Coverage:** Expanding healthcare coverage to include comprehensive services such as preventive care and mental health support is crucial for improving overall health outcomes. By investing in healthcare infrastructure, training healthcare professionals and increasing access to medical facilities, the government can ensure that citizens receive quality healthcare services.

4. **Quality Education for All:** Investing in public education and promoting access to higher education and skill-development opportunities can lead to a more educated and skilled workforce. Quality education equips individuals with the necessary tools to secure better employment opportunities, contributing to economic growth and development.

5. **Women-Empowerment Programs:** Empowering women through gender-specific initiatives is crucial for achieving gender equality and social development. Providing access to education, healthcare, financial services and entrepreneurship opportunities can help women actively participate in the economy and society.

6. **Nutrition and Food Security:** Strengthening food-security programs is vital for addressing malnutrition and ensuring adequate nutrition for vulnerable groups, especially pregnant women, infants and children. This can lead to improved health outcomes and overall well-being.

7. **Affordable Housing:** Addressing homelessness and improving living conditions for the urban and rural poor through affordable housing schemes is essential for promoting social

stability and economic development. Access to secure housing is a fundamental right and plays a crucial role in improving the quality of life for citizens.

8. **Enhanced Social Security:** Introducing comprehensive social-security measures, such as unemployment benefits and pensions, can protect citizens during economic uncertainties and in their old age. This provides a sense of security and dignity for individuals and families.

9. **Technology-Driven Delivery**: Leveraging technology for the efficient and transparent delivery of social-welfare programs can reduce leakages and ensure that benefits reach the intended beneficiaries. Digital platforms and direct-benefit-transfer mechanisms can streamline the delivery process and eliminate intermediaries.

10. **Community Participation:** Involving communities in the design and implementation of social-welfare programs ensures that initiatives are tailored to local needs and are sustainable. Community engagement fosters a sense of ownership and responsibility, making the programs more effective and impactful.

By undertaking these ten steps, India can enhance the effectiveness and impact of its social-welfare programs. Strengthening these programs is essential for promoting inclusive and sustainable development, reducing poverty and inequality and accelerating India's transformation into a developed nation by 2050. Prioritizing the well-being and empowerment of its citizens will contribute significantly to India's progress and standing as a compassionate and progressive nation on the global stage.

Conclusion

The statement emphasizes the importance of strengthening social-welfare programs in India to achieve a developed-nation status by 2050.

It highlights various key points such as tailoring welfare programs to specific needs, implementing poverty alleviation measures, ensuring universal basic services, providing comprehensive healthcare coverage, promoting women empowerment and gender equality, leveraging technology and digital platforms, fostering collaboration among stakeholders and conducting regular monitoring and evaluation to make evidence-based policy decisions and ensure the effectiveness of interventions. By investing in social welfare and addressing socio-economic disparities, India can create a more equitable and prosperous future and serve as an example for other nations pursuing inclusive development.

Promote Gender Equality

Introduction

Gender equality in India is about ensuring equal rights, opportunities and treatment for all genders, eliminating discrimination and biases. It aims to create a society where men and women have equal access to education, healthcare, employment and decision-making. This involves addressing various gender-related issues like promoting women empowerment, increasing female workforce participation, combating gender-based violence and eliminating harmful practices. By achieving gender equality, India can become more inclusive and equitable—benefiting the overall well-being and growth of the nation.

Defining Gender Equality

Gender equality in India is the principle of ensuring that everyone, regardless of their gender, is treated equally and has the same rights and opportunities in all aspects of life. It involves eradicating discrimination and biases based on gender, aiming to create a society where both men and women can access education, healthcare and employment, and participate in decision-making processes without any discrimination. Practically, achieving gender equality in India involves addressing various gender-related issues and challenges within the country. These efforts may include promoting women empowerment, encouraging greater female participation in the workforce, combating gender-based violence, ensuring fair pay for equal work and eliminating harmful practices like child marriage and female foeticide. By providing equal opportunities for all individuals to contribute to society and access resources, gender equality fosters a more inclusive and equitable society.

The Present State of Gender Equality in India and the Challenges before it

India, under the current government, has made significant progress in promoting gender equality and women empowerment through various initiatives and policies. These efforts encompass—creating legal reforms and educational schemes to support women; providing maternity support; increasing political representation for women; combatting gender-based violence; improving sanitary napkin accessibility and promoting digital literacy and skill development for female entrepreneurs. Despite these positive strides, challenges persist and progress may differ across regions and communities. Continued commitment to gender equality is vital for further advancements and the creation of a more equitable society. Despite commendable efforts in promoting gender equality in India, challenges like gender-based violence and the under-representation of women in decision-making roles are still rampant. To make substantial progress, continued efforts, effective policy implementation and public participation are essential. By empowering women and promoting gender equality, India can create a more inclusive and developed nation by 2050. This will unlock the full potential of all citizens, fostering sustainable and equitable growth for the country's future.

Measures to overcome the challenges of Gender Equality

To overcome the challenges of gender equality, India must implement various measures like executing comprehensive gender sensitization programs, strengthening legal reforms, empowering women through education, promoting the economic empowerment of women, addressing violence and safety issues, increasing the political representation of women, implementing supportive workplace policies, engaging communities, promoting responsible media representation and collecting gender-disaggregated data. These efforts will accelerate progress towards gender equality, fostering an inclusive society and driving India's long-term development and prosperity.

Promoting gender equality in India involves a multi-faceted approach with ten key strategies:

1. **Education and Awareness:** Develop gender-sensitive educational programs that challenge stereotypes and promote equal opportunities for boys and girls. Incorporate gender perspectives into curriculums, textbooks and teacher training.

2. **Economic Empowerment:** Enhance access to resources for women including credit and financial services, vocational training and support for women-led entrepreneurship.

3. **Equal Pay and Workplace Policies:** Enforce equal pay for equal work through labour law revisions, monitoring mechanisms and transparent pay scales. Encourage flexible work arrangements and work-life balance.

4. **Addressing Violence:** Strengthen the legal framework to address and prevent gender-based violence. Improve law enforcement, provide specialized training and establish support services for survivors.

5. **Political Empowerment:** Encourage the participation of women in politics through incentives like reserved seats in legislative bodies.

6. **Healthcare and Reproductive Rights:** Improve healthcare services, especially in underserved areas. Ensure access to family planning and reproductive health services.

7. **Digital Literacy:** Promote digital literacy among women and girls, offering training programs and affordable access to digital devices and the internet.

8. **Community Engagement:** Engage communities and raise awareness to challenge harmful gender norms and practices.

9. **Media Representation:** Promote gender-sensitive reporting and eliminate gender stereotypes in media content.

10. **Data Collection and Research:** Invest in collecting and analyzing gender-disaggregated data to design evidence-based policies and monitor progress.

Collaboration among the government, civil society and private sector is crucial for successful implementation. Empowering women leads to overall development and prosperity, as they become significant contributors to the nation's growth. Gender equality is linked to sustainable development as empowered women invest in their families' well-being and education. By embracing gender equality, India can create an inclusive society that benefits everyone—breaking down barriers and enabling individuals to reach their full potential for sustainable development.

Conclusion

Promoting gender equality is a crucial step for India to become a developed nation by 2050. Gender equality leads to economic growth through increased workforce participation, human capital development and poverty alleviation. It fosters inclusive governance, improves health and well-being, reduces gender-based violence and promotes digital transformation. Gender equality is closely linked to sustainable development and enhances India's global reputation. To achieve these goals, India must enforce gender-sensitive laws, provide equal opportunities in education and employment, promote the economic empowerment of women and address violence against women. By embracing gender equality, India can create a brighter and more equitable future—setting a positive example for other countries and realizing its vision of becoming a developed nation.

Invest in Science and Technology

Introduction

In the 21st century, India's journey towards becoming a developed nation relies heavily on strategic investment in science and technology. As a country with a vast and diverse population and a rapidly growing economy, India faces numerous challenges on its path to development. However, by placing a strong emphasis on science and technology, India can effectively tackle these challenges—fostering innovation, economic growth and social transformation. Through targeted investments in this field, India can secure a prosperous future, bridge the gap with developed nations and develop indigenous solutions to its unique problems. Embracing the power of innovation and research will elevate India to a prominent position on the global stage while significantly enhancing the well-being of its citizens.

Defining Science and Technology

Investing in science and technology refers to allocating financial resources and efforts towards research, development and the application of scientific knowledge and technological innovations. It plays a vital role in making India a developed nation by 2050 by driving economic growth; improving education, healthcare and infrastructure; promoting environmental sustainability; enhancing national security; fostering innovation and entrepreneurship and enabling global collaboration. Embracing science and technology leads to inclusive and sustainable development, positioning India as a developed nation on the global stage.

The Present State of Science and Technology in India and the Challenges before it

As of now, India has made significant progress in various scientific domains such as space research, IT, pharmaceuticals and renewable energy. Initiatives like 'Make in India', 'Digital India' and 'Startup India' have been introduced to promote innovation and research. The National Policy on Science and Technology outlines the roadmap for development. Funding has been increased for scientific institutions and projects, and international collaborations have been fostered.

Despite these achievements, challenges remain such as limited funding, collaboration and skill development. However, the government's emphasis on science and technology as drivers of growth and development is paving the way for a more innovative and technologically advanced India. Continuous efforts in research, development and education are crucial for India to become a global leader in science and technology and foster sustainable development and innovation.

To date, India has achieved significant progress in various scientific fields including space research, information technology, pharmaceuticals and renewable energy. The country's space agency, ISRO, has achieved remarkable milestones which include several successful satellite missions and reaching Mars with the Mars Orbiter Mission (Mangalyaan). India's IT sector has contributed significantly to the economy, and the pharmaceutical industry has become a global leader in producing generic drugs.

The government has actively supported research and development through initiatives and schemes like 'Make in India' and 'Startup

India', encouraging innovation and entrepreneurship. Despite these achievements, India faces challenges in its scientific landscape. Limited funding for research and development; lack of robust collaboration between academia, industry and the government and the need for greater investment in education and skill development are some of the challenges that need to be addressed.

To continue progress and become a global leader in science and technology, India must focus on sustained efforts in research, development and education. Strengthening collaborations, enhancing funding for R&D and investing in a skilled scientific workforce are crucial steps towards fostering sustainable development and innovation in the country. With continued dedication and investment, India can propel itself towards becoming a powerhouse in science and technology on the world stage.

Measures to overcome these Challenges

To overcome challenges in science and technology: India can increase funding for research and development, strengthen STEM education, establish technology transfer and incubation centres, foster public–private partnerships, implement supportive policies, promote international collaborations and focus on critical research areas. These measures will help India harness its scientific potential, drive innovation and position itself as a global leader in science and technology. This advancement will have a positive impact on various sectors and elevate India's status on the world stage.

To ensure investment in science and technology and make India a developed nation, the following ten strategies can be undertaken:

1. **Increase R&D Funding:** The government should allocate a higher percentage of GDP for research and development to encourage innovation and scientific breakthroughs. Investing

in cutting-edge research can lead to advancements in various sectors and drive economic growth.

2. **Promote Public–Private Partnerships:** Collaborations between government, industry and academia can enhance research, development and technology commercialization. Public–private partnerships bring together diverse expertise and resources, fostering a culture of innovation and driving real-world applications.

3. **Strengthen STEM Education:** Improve the quality of science, technology, engineering and mathematics education to foster a skilled workforce and nurture future innovators. Emphasizing STEM education from an early age equips students with critical thinking and problem-solving skills needed for scientific research and technological advancements.

4. **Establish Technology Incubation Centres:** Set up incubation centres to support start-ups and facilitate the conversion of research outcomes into marketable products. Incubation centres offer resources and mentorship and further provide funding to entrepreneurs—helping them turn innovative ideas into successful ventures.

5. **Focus on Critical Technologies**: Identify and prioritize critical areas such as artificial intelligence, biotechnology, renewable energy and space exploration for strategic investment. Targeted investment in these high-impact technologies can spur rapid advancements and boost India's competitiveness in the global arena.

6. **Attract Foreign Investment**: Create policies and incentives to attract foreign direct investment in research and technology sectors. Collaborating with international companies and institutions can facilitate knowledge exchange and access to global resources, driving technological progress.

7. **Encourage Innovation in MSMEs:** Provide financial support and incentives to Micro, Small and Medium Enterprises (MSMEs) to foster innovation and technology adoption. MSMEs play a crucial role in driving economic growth and job creation, as supporting innovation efforts can have significant impacts on the economy.

8. **Promote Digital Infrastructure:** Improve digital infrastructure and internet connectivity across the country to enable the widespread adoption of technology. Access to reliable and high-speed internet is essential for research, innovation and technology-driven businesses to thrive.

9. **Support Women in STEM:** Encourage and support the participation of women in science and technology fields to promote gender diversity and inclusivity. Empowering women in STEM not only benefits individuals but also leads to diverse perspectives and better problem-solving in research and innovation.

10. **Facilitate Technology Transfer:** Establish mechanisms to transfer technology from research institutions to industries for commercialization. Streamlining the technology transfer process can bridge the gap between research outcomes and practical applications, stimulating economic growth and technological advancements.

By implementing these strategies, India can create an ecosystem that promotes scientific research, technological advancements and innovation. Investment in science and technology will lead to economic growth, job creation, improved healthcare, sustainable development and overall progress, thus propelling India towards becoming a developed nation by 2050. Embracing science and technology as strategic pillars of national development will be crucial in overcoming challenges and unlocking the full potential of the nation's human capital and resources.

Conclusion

In conclusion, India's path towards becoming a developed nation by 2050 hinges on investing in science and technology. This strategic imperative will unlock India's full potential, driving progress and prosperity across various sectors. By advancing healthcare, agriculture, energy and the environment—India can enhance the well-being of its citizens and contribute to sustainable development. To achieve these goals, increased R&D funding and collaborations between academia, industry and international partners are essential. A robust science and technology education system will nurture a skilled workforce capable of driving innovation and research. Prioritizing emerging technologies and promoting science communication will lead to transformative advancements in various fields. India's space program will achieve remarkable milestones, and digital transformation will streamline governance for greater efficiency and citizen engagement.

Crucially, these investments will prioritize social inclusion—empowering marginalized communities. Leveraging its human capital and talent, India will emerge as a global leader in research and development, ready to tackle future challenges and seize growth opportunities. Future India, in 2050, will be technologically advanced, sustainable and inclusive—with science and technology as the driving force behind its transformation into a developed nation.

Foster Cultural Preservation

Introduction

Cultural preservation is of utmost importance for India's development as it fosters national unity, social cohesion and community-centric progress. The diverse cultural heritage—encompassing languages, traditions, arts, music, dance, architecture and belief systems—creates a vibrant national identity. Preserving this heritage not only connects people across backgrounds but also promotes integration. India's traditional knowledge in fields like medicine, agriculture and craftsmanship can offer sustainable solutions, driving community-centric development.

Cultural sites and arts contribute to cultural tourism, fuelling economic growth. Integrating cultural knowledge into education enhances the youth's understanding and appreciation of India's heritage. Showcasing cultural richness on the global stage enhances India's soft power and international influence, attracting collaborations and investments. Ultimately, cultural preservation safeguards India's past and paves the way for a prosperous future, thus playing a pivotal role in its journey towards becoming a developed country.

Defining Cultural Preservation

Cultural preservation is essential for India's development into a developed nation by 2050. It involves safeguarding traditional heritage, knowledge and practices—fostering national identity, social cohesion and pride. Preserving traditional knowledge contributes to finding sustainable solutions, while cultural richness attracts tourists—boosting the economy. Integrating cultural knowledge in education inspires the youth while showcasing heritage enhances global recognition and soft power. In addition to these, cultural preservation supports eco-friendly and community-centric development. In summary, cultural preservation plays a significant role in India's journey towards becoming a developed country by 2050.

The efforts of the present Government to Foster Cultural Preservation

India has undertaken commendable initiatives to preserve its cultural heritage. The efforts include conserving historical monuments; supporting traditional arts, literature and languages; digitizing ancient texts; promoting UNESCO World Heritage Sites; organizing cultural festivals; promoting yoga and Ayurveda and engaging in cultural exchanges. Challenges like urbanization and lack of funding persist, requiring sustained and collaborative efforts from the government, civil society and individuals to safeguard and promote India's diverse cultural legacy for future generations.

The efforts needed to Foster Cultural Preservation

To foster cultural preservation in India, various measures are essential. Strengthening legislation to protect cultural sites and heritage is crucial, along with raising public awareness, especially among the younger generation. Engaging local communities and fostering public–private partnerships are vital for safeguarding traditional knowledge and promoting India's cultural legacy. Leveraging technology for digitization and promoting sustainable tourism practices are effective ways to preserve cultural artefacts and sites while benefiting local communities economically. Investing in capacity building for local communities and collaborating internationally can further enhance India's cultural preservation efforts and showcase its richness on the global stage. By implementing these measures, India can effectively promote social cohesion, sustainable tourism and global recognition while cherishing its diverse cultural heritage.

Public–private partnerships provide additional resources and expertise while harnessing technology aids in documentation and preservation. Promoting sustainable tourism prioritizes cultural heritage preservation while also supporting local economies. Investing in capacity building for professionals involved in cultural preservation enhances their skills, while documentation and research ensure continuity for future generations. International collaborations and interdisciplinary approaches further strengthen India's cultural preservation efforts. By adopting these measures, India can sustainably safeguard its diverse cultural heritage, promoting national identity and history, while also enhancing its global standing as a culturally rich nation.

The 10 Steps that India can undertake to ensure Cultural Preservation

1. **Strengthen Legal Frameworks:** Implement and enforce stringent laws and policies to protect cultural heritage sites, artefacts and traditions. Robust legal frameworks will safeguard India's diverse cultural legacy.

2. **Promote Public Awareness:** Launch extensive public awareness campaigns, educational programs and media initiatives to instil pride and appreciation for India's cultural heritage, especially among the youth.

3. **Involve Local Communities:** Engage and empower local communities in the preservation and management of cultural heritage, tapping into their traditional knowledge and practices to ensure effective conservation.

4. **Encourage Public–Private Partnerships:** Foster collaborations between the government, private sector and civil society organizations to pool resources, expertise and funding for cultural preservation projects.

5. **Embrace Technology and Innovation:** Utilize advanced technologies such as 3D scanning, virtual reality and digital archiving to document, restore and preserve cultural artefacts and heritage sites.

6. **Promote Sustainable Tourism:** Implement sustainable tourism practices that prioritize the preservation of cultural heritage while generating economic benefits for local communities.

7. **Invest in Capacity Building:** Provide training and capacity-building programs for professionals involved in cultural preservation, including archaeologists, conservators and museum curators.

8. **Document and Research Cultural Practices:** Conduct thorough research and documentation of cultural practices, rituals and traditional knowledge to ensure their preservation and transmission to future generations.

9. **Collaborate Internationally:** Engage in international collaborations and partnerships with global organizations to gain support, resources and knowledge sharing for cultural preservation initiatives.

10. **Adopt Interdisciplinary Approaches:** Encourage collaborations between experts from various fields–such as archaeology, history, anthropology and technology—to develop comprehensive and effective cultural preservation strategies.

By undertaking these steps, India can foster cultural preservation and celebrate its rich heritage while advancing towards becoming a developed nation. Embracing its cultural diversity and history will not only strengthen national identity but also contribute to social cohesion, sustainable tourism and elevate India's soft power and influence on the global stage. Cultural preservation will play a pivotal role in shaping a prosperous and culturally rich India in the years to come.

Conclusion

In 2050, Future India will be a nation that embraces cultural preservation and celebrates its diverse heritage. It will protect historical sites, revitalize traditional arts, promote regional languages and engage in responsible cultural tourism. Utilizing technology for preservation and virtual experiences, Future India will encourage community participation and international collaboration. The cultural renaissance will sustain India's identity while enriching global cultural understanding. Future India will be a vibrant and inclusive nation cherishing its rich cultural tapestry.

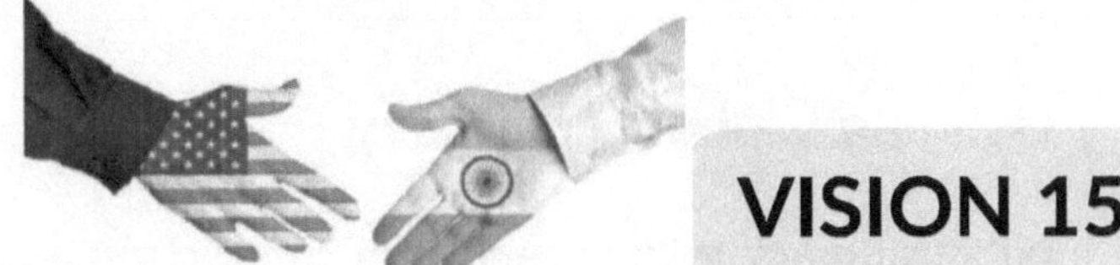

Enhance Global Diplomacy

Introduction

Enhancing global diplomacy is vital for India's development, providing economic growth through foreign investments, resource access and technology exchange. Collaborating with other countries on counter-terrorism and environmental protection ensures global stability and secures India's security and sustainable development. Cultural diplomacy and soft power are essential for projecting a positive image of India worldwide, attracting tourism and fostering goodwill. Engaging in global diplomacy enables India to contribute to humanitarian efforts and promote peace and stability regionally and internationally.

Participating in international forums empowers India to advocate for its development goals and assert its interests globally. Building strong diplomatic relationships positions India as a responsible global player and influencer in international affairs, fostering mutual progress and benefits. Overall, strengthening global diplomacy is a strategic imperative for India's journey towards becoming a developed nation and a respected global leader. It facilitates economic growth, technology advancement, security cooperation and environmental sustainability while projecting a positive image of India on the world stage.

Defining Global Diplomacy

Global diplomacy is the practice of conducting international relations and negotiations between nations and international organizations to promote peace, cooperation and mutual interests. In the context of making India a developed nation by 2050, global diplomacy plays a crucial role. It allows India to foster economic growth by attracting foreign investments and accessing resources and technology. Diplomatic efforts also address security threats, work on global challenges and promote cultural exchange, all of which enhance India's global standing and soft power.

Engaging in multilateral forums through global diplomacy enables India to advocate for its development goals and interests on the international stage. It also allows India to provide humanitarian aid and contribute to global efforts in areas such as environmental protection and peacekeeping. Through effective diplomatic engagement, India can achieve economic prosperity, technological advancements, national security and global cooperation, all of which contribute to its development and progress as a developed nation by 2050.

The Present State of global diplomacy in India and the Challenges before it

In recent years, India has undertaken various measures to enhance its global diplomacy and strengthen its position in the international community. These efforts include engaging in bilateral and multilateral dialogues with other nations and international organizations, prioritizing neighbourhood diplomacy to strengthen relations with neighbouring countries and intensifying engagement with Southeast Asian nations through the Act East Policy. Strategic partnerships with major powers like the United States, Japan and European countries have been established, encompassing areas such as defence, trade, technology and security.

Participation in global forums like the United Nations, G20, BRICS and SCO has enabled India to advocate for its interests and actively contribute to global decision-making. During the COVID-19 pandemic, India demonstrated its commitment to global cooperation by providing humanitarian aid and COVID-19 vaccines to several countries.

Furthermore, India has pursued economic and trade agreements with various countries and regional blocs to expand economic opportunities and diversify its trade portfolio. Collaboration on renewable-energy projects, climate initiatives and involvement in forums like the International Solar Alliance showcase India's dedication to energy and climate cooperation. The country also promotes cultural diplomacy by hosting international events, cultural festivals and facilitating educational exchanges for foreign students. The Indian diaspora plays a significant role in enhancing India's global diplomacy, and the government actively engages with them to leverage their connections and influence in other countries. Overall, India's efforts in global diplomacy continue to evolve—with a focus on fostering cooperation, strengthening ties and contributing to global development and prosperity.

The present state of global diplomacy in India demonstrates an active and dynamic approach to international relations. India engages with countries worldwide and participates in multilateral forums to promote its interests, contribute to global issues and strengthen its global standing. However, there are various challenges in further enhancing India's global diplomacy which include geopolitical complexities, border disputes, trade imbalances, climate change and health-related concerns.

Measures to overcome these challenges

To overcome these challenges and enhance global diplomacy, India can undertake several measures. These include diversifying diplomatic engagement, strengthening regional cooperation, implementing economic reforms, taking a leadership role in climate initiatives, leveraging healthcare capabilities for global health initiatives, actively participating in multilateral forums, promoting soft power and focusing on science and technology diplomacy.

The 10 Steps that India can undertake to ensure global diplomacy and become a developed county

To enhance global diplomacy and strengthen India's position as a developed country by 2050, the following ten steps can be undertaken:

1. **Strengthen Diplomatic Corps:** Invest in training and capacity building of diplomats to enhance negotiation skills, language proficiency and cultural understanding—enabling them to effectively represent India's interests on the global stage.

2. **Diversify Diplomatic Alliances:** Actively engage with a diverse set of nations and regions to build strategic partnerships and foster economic, technological and cultural collaborations for India's development.

3. **Focus on Economic Diplomacy:** Prioritize economic diplomacy to attract foreign investments, promote trade and access technology—enabling India's economic growth and industrial development.

4. **Develop Soft-Power Initiatives:** Promote India's soft power through cultural exchanges, educational partnerships and cultural festivals—enhancing its global reputation and appeal.

5. **Participate Actively in Multilateral Forums:** Engage actively in international organizations like the United Nations, G20, BRICS and ASEAN to advocate for India's interests and contribute to shaping global policies.

6. **Address Global Challenges Collaboratively:** Collaborate with other nations to address global challenges like climate change,

sustainable development and counter-terrorism—showcasing India's commitment to global cooperation.

7. **Leverage Digital Diplomacy:** Utilize digital platforms, social media and virtual conferences to connect with global audiences, disseminate India's perspectives and engage in diplomatic dialogues.

8. **Focus on Track-II Diplomacy:** Strengthen track-II diplomacy by encouraging dialogues between non-governmental actors, academics and think tanks to foster deeper understanding and cooperation between nations.

9. **Promote People-to-People Contacts:** Facilitate exchanges of students, professionals and artists to promote cultural understanding, mutual learning and collaboration between India and other countries.

10. **Strategic Public Diplomacy Campaigns:** Design and implement strategic public diplomacy campaigns to communicate India's vision, achievements and contributions to the world—projecting India as a responsible global partner.

By undertaking these steps, India can enhance its global diplomacy, forge strong alliances, address global challenges and leverage its cultural heritage and soft power to propel its development as a developed nation by 2050. An assertive and proactive approach to global diplomacy will position India as a key player in the international arena—driving economic growth, technological advancements and social progress for a prosperous future.

Conclusion

In conclusion, enhancing global diplomacy is essential for India's development and global prominence by 2050. By actively engaging with nations worldwide, forming strategic partnerships and promoting its cultural heritage and technological advancements, India can emerge as a major global power and a respected leader in shaping international affairs. India's diplomatic efforts, as demonstrated through policies like the Act East Policy and Neighbourhood First Policy, reflect its commitment to regional stability and cooperation. Active participation in multilateral forums showcases India's growing diplomatic influence and dedication to responsible global engagement.

Looking ahead, India's continued focus on global diplomacy is expected to yield significant results—fostering economic growth, regional stability and a strong global leadership position. By prioritizing strategic partnerships, global connectivity, humanitarian assistance and cultural and technological diplomacy, India can contribute positively to global peace, stability and prosperity—fostering a more inclusive and cooperative world order. By embracing the opportunities and challenges of global diplomacy, India can navigate the complexities of the international landscape and emerge as a developed nation with a robust global presence by 2050.

Improve Ease-of-doing-business

Introduction

Improving the ease-of-doing-business is crucial for India's economic growth and development. By creating a business-friendly environment through reforms like reducing bureaucracy and enhancing regulatory efficiency, India can attract investments, stimulate economic activity and foster job creation. These advantages extend to both large corporations and small to medium enterprises, contributing to inclusive growth. Moreover, streamlining the business environment will bolster India's global image as an attractive investment destination and showcase its potential for sustainable development and prosperity. Embracing reforms to improve the ease-of-doing-business is a pivotal step towards unlocking India's economic potential and positioning it as a dynamic and prosperous nation on the global stage.

Defining Ease-of-doing-business

The ease-of-doing-business refers to the convenience and efficiency with which businesses can operate within a country. It encompasses various factors such as starting a business, obtaining permits, accessing credit and more. Improving the ease-of-doing-business is crucial for India's development as it directly impacts economic growth, job creation and entrepreneurship. By attracting more investments and fostering a business-friendly environment, India can promote economic growth, enhance competitiveness and drive innovation. Furthermore, streamlined business procedures will contribute to increased government revenue, poverty reduction and sustainable development. Embracing reforms to improve ease-of-doing-business will play a pivotal role in accelerating India's path towards becoming a developed nation by 2050, ensuring inclusive prosperity and a positive global reputation.

The Present State of Ease-of-Doing-Business in India and the Challenges Before it

In recent years, the Indian government has undertaken significant measures to improve the Ease-of-doing-business in the country. These include implementing the Goods and Services Tax (GST), enacting the Insolvency and Bankruptcy Code (IBC) and simplifying company registration through online processes. Digital platforms and single-window clearance mechanisms have been established to streamline bureaucratic procedures. Labour and banking reforms have been initiated to facilitate access to credit and simplify labour compliance. As a result of these efforts, India has experienced improvements in its Ease-of-doing-business rankings. However, continuous reforms are needed to create an investor-friendly environment and further enhance the ease-of-doing-business. By reducing bureaucratic hurdles and promoting transparency, India can attract more investments, promote entrepreneurship and drive economic growth—contributing to its development as a nation.

Measures to overcome these challenges

To overcome the challenges before the ease-of-doing-business and make India a developed nation, the government and policymakers should focus on implementing regulatory reforms, accelerating digital transformation, investing in infrastructure, improving land acquisition processes, strengthening contract enforcement, modernizing labour laws, simplifying the tax system, offering investor-friendly policies and enhancing the capacity of government officials and institutions. By addressing these challenges and implementing the suggested measures, India can attract more investments, promote entrepreneurship and create a conducive environment for businesses to thrive. This will contribute significantly to India's overall economic development and growth, paving the way for its transformation into a developed nation.

10 Strategies that India can undertake to improve ease-of-doing-business to become a developed country by 2050:

To achieve the goal of becoming a developed country by 2050, India needs to undertake ten key strategies to ensure ease-of-doing-business and create a conducive environment for businesses to thrive:

1. **Streamline Regulations:** Simplifying and rationalizing business regulations are crucial to reduce bureaucratic complexities and provide clarity to businesses. This can involve eliminating redundant or contradictory rules, creating a single-window system for approvals and digitizing regulatory processes.

2. **Digital Transformation:** Embracing digital technologies can revolutionize government services and administrative processes. By offering online portals for business registration, permit applications and compliance filings, India can significantly reduce paperwork, processing times and corruption.

3. **Infrastructure Development:** Investment in modern infrastructure is vital for seamless business operations. Efficient transportation networks, reliable energy supply, robust communication systems and well-developed logistics facilities will enhance productivity and competitiveness.

4. **Land Reforms:** Efficient land acquisition processes and clear land titles are essential to attract investments. Implementing a transparent and expedited land acquisition system, along with

robust land-use change approvals, will remove barriers for businesses.

5. **Contract Enforcement:** A strong legal system and specialized commercial courts are critical for enforcing contracts and resolving disputes efficiently. Speedy and fair dispute resolution mechanisms instil confidence in businesses and investors.

6. **Labour Reforms:** Modernizing labour laws can strike a balance between worker rights and ease-of-doing-business. Flexible labour laws can encourage formal employment and provide businesses with the agility to adapt to market demands.

7. **Tax Simplification:** Continuously simplifying the tax system, unifying tax rates and reducing compliance burdens will make India more attractive for businesses. A predictable and stable tax regime fosters investor confidence and facilitates business planning.

8. **Investor-Friendly Policies:** Offering incentives and support for investments in strategic sectors can attract both domestic and foreign investors. Targeted policies can create a favourable climate for specific industries and encourage long-term investments.

9. **Capacity Building:** Enhancing the skills and capabilities of government officials is essential for the successful implementation of reforms. Adequately trained and competent officials can ensure that reforms are executed efficiently and effectively.

10. **Strengthen Institutions:** Ensuring the independence and effectiveness of regulatory bodies and institutions is vital for transparency and accountability in governance. Strong and credible institutions create a stable and predictable regulatory environment for businesses.

By implementing these ten steps, India can create a business-friendly ecosystem that attracts investments, promotes entrepreneurship and fosters economic growth. A conducive business environment will lead to increased job opportunities, higher productivity and overall socio-economic development—ultimately propelling India towards its goal of becoming a developed nation by 2050. These strategies will be pivotal in transforming India into a globally competitive, dynamic and prosperous nation.

Conclusion

Improving the ease-of-doing-business is a crucial factor for India's development and its journey towards becoming a developed nation by 2050. Streamlining regulations, embracing digital transformation, investing in infrastructure and implementing efficient land and labour reforms are essential steps to attract investments, boost entrepreneurship and stimulate economic growth. This will lead to job creation, enhanced productivity and innovation while encouraging businesses to operate formally and comply with regulations. The simplified and transparent business environment will reduce bureaucracy and corruption, making it easier for businesses to operate and flourish. Economic development will generate revenue for the government, which can be reinvested in social welfare and infrastructure development. Enhanced ease-of-doing-business will positively impact various sectors, leading to overall socio-economic development and improved living standards for citizens. India envisions a future as a competitive player in the global market—a beacon of prosperity and opportunity.

Promote Digitalization

Introduction

Promoting digitalization is crucial for India's development in the rapidly evolving digital age. Integrating digital technologies into various aspects of society, economy and governance can unlock opportunities and propel India towards becoming a developed nation. Digitalization can boost economic growth, foster financial inclusion, streamline governance, revolutionize education and healthcare, drive infrastructure development, spur innovation, support entrepreneurship and promote environmental sustainability. Embracing digital technologies empowers India to leverage its demographic dividend and technological potential, accelerating development and positioning itself as a global leader in the digital era.

Define Promoting digitalization

Promoting digitalization involves adopting and integrating digital technologies to drive economic growth, improve governance and empower citizens. It plays a significant role in making India a developed nation by 2050

Embracing digitalization is essential for India as it leads to economic growth, inclusive development, efficient governance, advancement in healthcare, sustainable development, education revolution, smart infrastructure, digital entrepreneurship, global competitiveness and a skilled workforce. By building a digitally adept nation, India can ensure the well-being and prosperity of its citizens in the digital age and achieve inclusive and sustainable development, ultimately positioning itself as a developed nation by 2050.

The Present State of digitalization in India and the Challenges before it

The present government of India has implemented various initiatives to promote digitalization and harness digital technologies for economic growth, efficient governance and improved service delivery. The key initiative is 'Digital India', which aims to provide digital infrastructure, literacy and services to all citizens. The Aadhaar program assigns a unique biometric number to each resident, facilitating various digital services. BHIM UPI enables instant and secure money transfers between bank accounts through mobile phones. The GSTN streamlines taxation processes, while other digital payment initiatives promote cashless transactions. 'Make in India' for Electronics focuses on local production of electronic goods, while 'Startup India' supports and incentivizes start-ups. The National Digital Health Mission (NDHM) connects stakeholders through digital health records; the National Broadband Mission (NBM) enhances rural digital connectivity while several Digital literacy programs empower citizens with technical skills. These efforts demonstrate India's commitment to inclusive and sustainable development through digital transformation.

India has made substantial progress in promoting digitalization through various initiatives. The key achievements include the 'Digital India' Initiative, the Aadhaar biometric identity system, the Unified Payments Interface (UPI) for digital payments and the JAM Trinity, which combines Jan Dhan Yojana, Aadhaar and Mobile phones to improve welfare delivery. The country's start-up ecosystem has thrived, aided by initiatives like 'Startup India'. Digital education, Smart

Cities Mission, digital healthcare and the National Knowledge Network have also played pivotal roles in transforming India into a digitally empowered society. These efforts demonstrate India's commitment to leveraging digital technology for the betterment of society and align with its vision of becoming a developed nation by 2050.

Measures to overcome these Challenges

India has made significant progress in digitalization, with improvements in internet penetration, widespread digital payments, enhanced e-governance, a thriving start-up ecosystem and efforts to promote digital skills. However, challenges like the urban–rural digital divide, cyber-security risks, data privacy concerns, digital illiteracy, infrastructure development and regulatory complexities still exist. To further advance digitalization, suggested measures include expanding rural internet access, enhancing digital literacy programs, investing in cyber security, enacting data protection laws, fostering skill development, supporting start-ups, promoting digital payments, expanding e-governance and conducting public awareness campaigns. Promoting digitalization in India is crucial for its development and journey towards becoming a developed country by 2050.

10 Strategies by which India can promote Digitalization

Here are ten strategies that India can adopt to promote digitalization effectively:

1. **Universal Internet Access:** Expand internet infrastructure to rural and remote areas for universal internet access, bridging the urban–rural digital divide.

2. **Digital Literacy Programs:** Implement comprehensive digital literacy programs to educate citizens of all age groups, including marginalized communities, on using digital technologies effectively and safely.

3. **Cyber-security Measures:** Strengthen cyber-security protocols to protect against cyber-threats and ensure the safety of users' data and digital transactions.

4. **Data Protection Laws:** Enact and enforce robust data protection laws to safeguard user data and build trust in digital services.

5. **Skill-Development Initiatives:** Invest in skill-development programs to train the workforce in emerging technologies, fostering a digitally competent and innovative workforce.

6. **E-Governance Expansion:** Expand user-friendly e-governance services to enhance transparency, efficiency and accessibility in government operations.

7. **Digital Payments Promotion:** Encourage the adoption of digital payment systems to reduce reliance on cash transactions and promote financial inclusion.

8. **Investment in Digital Infrastructure:** Continuously invest in digital infrastructure, including broadband connectivity, to support seamless digital services.

9. **Start-up and Innovation Support:** Foster a conducive ecosystem for start-ups and digital innovation by providing financial support and favourable regulatory frameworks.

10. **Public Awareness Campaigns:** Conduct awareness campaigns to educate citizens about the benefits and safe usage of digital technologies, encouraging greater adoption.

By implementing these strategies, India can create an inclusive and sustainable digital ecosystem that contributes significantly to the nation's development and economic growth.

Conclusion

In conclusion, promoting digitalization is crucial for India's development and its vision of becoming a developed nation by 2050. Embracing digital technology, enhancing digital literacy and promoting e-governance initiatives can revolutionize public service delivery, improve efficiency and enhance transparency. By investing in digital infrastructure, skill development and innovation, India can drive economic growth, financial inclusion and sustainable development. Moreover, digitalization can improve healthcare, education and governance—leading to a technologically advanced and inclusive society. The government, in collaboration with various stakeholders, should work towards creating an enabling environment for digitalization, prioritizing infrastructure development, cyber security and digital literacy. By harnessing the transformative power of digitalization, India can position itself as a leading global player and achieve its aspirations of becoming a developed nation by 2050.

Invest in Defence and Security

Introduction

Defence and security are crucial for India's development as they safeguard national sovereignty, contribute to peace and stability regionally and globally, attract investments and drive technological advancements. Furthermore, they enable efficient disaster response and humanitarian aid, elevate India's global standing and foster social progress. While investing in defence is important, it should be balanced with social-welfare spending to ensure holistic nation-building. Overall, a robust defence posture empowers India to build a prosperous and resilient nation, positively impacting global peace and prosperity.

Defining Defence and Security and its Importance for India

Defence and security are interconnected concepts aimed at safeguarding a nation from external and internal threats—ensuring sovereignty, peace and stability. Defence involves military measures to protect against aggression and defend national interests, while security encompasses a broader range of protection efforts—addressing various threats such as terrorism, cyber-attacks, disasters and social unrest. Both defence and security are vital for ensuring the safety and well-being of a nation's citizens and maintaining its resilience and prosperity. Defence and security are crucial for India's development and progress towards becoming a developed nation. They protect the country from external and internal threats—ensuring sovereignty, peace and stability. Investing in defence offers several benefits for India.

A strategic focus on defence and security is essential for India's development and progress as a prosperous and developed nation. It ensures national sovereignty by protecting borders and enabling independent decision-making. Defence investments contribute to regional and global stability, fostering diplomatic relations and reducing conflict risks. A secure environment attracts investments, leading to economic growth and job opportunities. Moreover, the defence sector drives technological advancements with civilian applications, enhancing overall technological progress. A well-equipped defence enables efficient disaster response, ensuring citizen safety and rapid recovery during emergencies. Furthermore, a strong defence enhances India's global influence, allowing active participation in international efforts. A secure environment also supports social progress by improving education, healthcare and social welfare—leading to better citizen well-being. Together, these factors empower India to become a developed nation.

The Present State of investment in defence and security in India and the Challenges before it

The Indian government has initiated various measures to invest in the defence and security of the country. These initiatives encompass:

1. **Modernizing Armed Forces:** Upgrading defence equipment and technology—including fighter jets, submarines, artillery, missiles and surveillance systems—to enhance operational capabilities.

2. **Promoting Indigenous Defence Production:** Encouraging domestic defence manufacturing through initiatives like 'Make in India' to reduce reliance on imports and enhance self-sufficiency.

3. **Strengthening Cyber security:** Bolstering capabilities to safeguard critical infrastructure and data from cyber-threats.

4. **Developing Border Infrastructure:** Improving infrastructure along international boundaries to enhance border security and mobility.

5. **Enhancing Coastal Security:** Strengthening surveillance and patrolling to counter maritime threats and piracy.

6. **Improving Counterterrorism Efforts:** Enhancing counterterrorism capabilities through intelligence cooperation and specialized units.

7. **Capacity Building and Training:** Providing specialized training and exercises to enhance the skills and readiness of armed forces and security personnel.

8. **Allocations in Defence Budget:** Increasing the defence budget to meet security challenges and modernization requirements.

9. **Defence Cooperation with Other Nations:** Engaging in joint military exercises and defence cooperation to foster strategic partnerships.

10. **National-Security Policy and Reforms:** Formulating comprehensive policies and reforms to address evolving security challenges effectively.

India faces multiple challenges in strengthening its defence and security:

1. **Geopolitical Complexity:** Dealing with border disputes, regional instability and security concerns with neighbouring countries presents significant challenges.

2. **Technological Gap:** Bridging the technological disparity with advanced military powers is a crucial area that requires improvement.

3. **Defence Procurement Delays:** Delays in defence procurement processes hinder the timely acquisition of critical equipment and technology.

4. **Budget Constraints:** Despite increased defence budget allocation, financial limitations can impact the pace of modernization efforts.

5. **Coordination among Agencies:** Enhancing coordination and collaboration among different defence and security agencies is essential for effective responses to security threats.

The Measures needed to overcome these challenges

To overcome the challenges and improve defence and security, India must undertake several measures—including streamlining defence procurements, boosting indigenous research and development, strengthening cyber security, modernizing military training, enhancing diplomatic ties, collaborating with strategic partners, bolstering maritime security, implementing national-security reforms, promoting public–private partnerships in defence and prioritizing interagency cooperation. These actions aim to address emerging threats and foster a more secure and resilient nation. However, it is essential to acknowledge that defence and security challenges are dynamic and that the government's strategies have progressed to a great extent. (For the latest information, official sources and news outlets should be consulted.)

10 Strategies by which India can invest in Defence and Security to become a developed nation

1. **Modernization and Indigenous R&D:** To become a developed nation, India must invest in modernizing its armed forces with advanced defence equipment and technology. Acquiring state-of-the-art fighter jets, submarines, artillery, missiles and surveillance systems will enhance the operational capabilities of the military. Simultaneously, promoting indigenous research

and development is crucial to reduce reliance on imports and bolster self-sufficiency in defence production. Initiatives like 'Make in India' can boost domestic defence manufacturing, fostering technological innovation and economic growth.

2. **Strengthen Border Security:** India's geopolitical complexities require a strong focus on improving border security. Investing in the enhancement of border infrastructure and surveillance capabilities along international boundaries is imperative to safeguard national security and protect territorial integrity. Developing border outposts, installing advanced surveillance systems and enhancing patrolling will bolster India's defence capabilities.

3. **Cyber-security Enhancement:** In the digital age, cyber security is critical for national security. India needs to strengthen its cyber-security measures to safeguard critical infrastructure and sensitive data from cyber-threats. This entails building robust cyber-defence systems, investing in advanced cyber-security technologies and enhancing the capabilities of cyber-security personnel. Collaborating with the private sector and academia can further strengthen India's cyber-security capabilities.

4. **Counterterrorism Measures:** India faces challenges from various terrorist groups, making specialized counterterrorism units and robust intelligence capabilities essential. Investing in advanced training, intelligence gathering and counterterrorism operations will enable India to effectively prevent and respond to terrorist threats—ensuring internal security and stability.

5. **Increase Defence Budget Allocation:** To invest in defence and security, India must ensure a steady increase in defence budget allocation. A well-funded defence sector can meet modernization needs, procure state-of-the-art equipment and address evolving security challenges effectively. Allocating a

significant portion of the budget to defence will demonstrate the country's commitment to national security and development.

6. **Defence Procurement Reforms:** Streamlining defence procurement processes is crucial to expedite acquisitions and reduce delays in acquiring critical defence equipment and technology. Transparent and efficient procurement systems can facilitate timely upgrades of the armed forces and ensure the quick deployment of modern weaponry and technology.

7. **Military Training and Capacity Building:** Enhancing military training methodologies and facilities is essential for ensuring the armed forces' operational readiness and efficiency. Regular and advanced training programs—including joint exercises with friendly nations—can improve the skills and readiness of soldiers, making them more effective in their roles.

8. **Strategic Partnerships:** Collaborating with strategic partners in defence can provide India access to advanced defence technology and expertise. Engaging in joint military exercises, defence cooperation and technology transfers can strengthen India's defence capabilities and foster international cooperation. Strategic partnerships with key nations can enhance India's global standing and security.

9. **Maritime Security Enhancement:** With an extensive coastline and maritime interests, strengthening coastal security measures and enhancing naval capabilities is crucial. Investments in modern naval vessels, coastal surveillance systems and patrolling will safeguard India's maritime borders and interests—including those in the Indian Ocean region.

10. **Interagency Coordination:** Effective responses to security threats require seamless coordination and collaboration among various defence and security agencies. Improved interagency coordination fosters synergy, enhances intelligence sharing and enables a more comprehensive approach to address security

challenges. Enhancing coordination between the armed forces, intelligence agencies, law enforcement and other security bodies will lead to a more cohesive and efficient defence and security ecosystem.

By implementing these ten strategies, India can bolster its defence and security capabilities, which are vital for ensuring national sovereignty, safeguarding citizens and contributing to regional stability. A strong defence and security framework will also foster investor confidence, promote economic growth and pave the way for India's development as a developed nation by 2050. As security challenges continue to evolve in the dynamic global landscape, India must continually adapt and innovate to maintain its position as a resilient and secure nation.

Conclusion

Investing in defence and security is essential for India's development as a developed nation by 2050. A strong defence deters adversaries, safeguards territorial integrity and boosts investor confidence—fostering economic growth. It enables effective responses to challenges like terrorism and cyber-threats, promoting indigenous defence manufacturing and research. Furthermore, a robust defence enhances regional stability, improves diplomatic standing and positively impacts global affairs. Overall, defence investment sets the foundation for stability, prosperity, innovation and citizen well-being—ensuring India's progress towards its developmental goals.

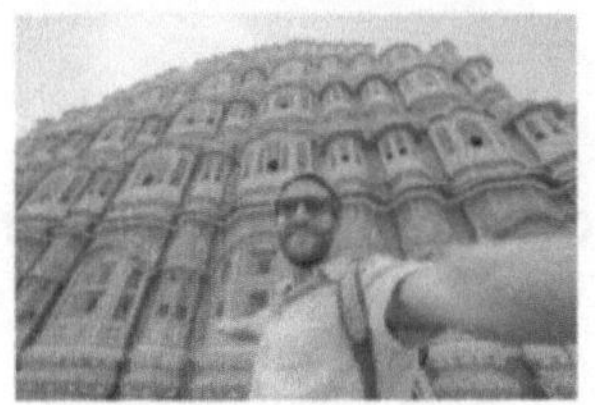

Promote Tourism

Introduction

Promoting tourism is crucial for India's development as a developed nation by 2050. Tourism offers numerous benefits including economic growth through foreign exchange earnings and job creation. It also fosters cultural preservation, cross-cultural understanding and infrastructure development. A thriving tourism sector enhances India's global image, attracts foreign investments and promotes sustainability. Improved connectivity and cultural diplomacy further contribute to India's journey towards becoming a developed nation while celebrating its diverse heritage and fostering international connections.

Moreover, tourism contributes to employment generation, particularly in rural areas, thereby aiding in poverty alleviation and fostering inclusive growth. By showcasing its rich cultural heritage and historical sites, tourism also supports cultural preservation and encourages sustainable practices. Furthermore, tourism acts as a catalyst for global cooperation and understanding, positioning India as a welcoming and inclusive destination. With a strategic approach and responsible practices, India can harness its diverse cultural and natural resources to propel its journey towards becoming a developed nation, while also embracing its unique identity and engaging with the global community.

Defining Tourism and its role in making India a developed nation

Tourism is the activity of travelling for leisure, recreation or exploration to various destinations—both within a country and internationally. It involves individuals or groups visiting places to experience different cultures, historical sites and natural attractions; and engage in recreational activities.

Tourism's diverse role in making India a developed nation includes contributing to economic growth, job creation, cultural preservation, cross-cultural understanding, infrastructure development and global image enhancement; attracting foreign investments; promoting sustainability; improving connectivity and fostering cultural diplomacy. By strategically promoting responsible tourism, India can leverage these advantages to achieve its development goals while celebrating its unique identity and engaging with the global community.

The Present State of Tourism in India and the Challenges before it

India, under the present government, has taken several proactive steps to promote tourism and recognize its potential for economic growth and development. Here are some key initiatives:

1. **Incredible India Campaign:** The government launched the 'Incredible India' campaign to showcase India's rich cultural, historical and natural heritage to the world—positioning it as a preferred global tourist destination.

2. **E-Visa Facility:** India introduced e-visa facilities for citizens of over 170 countries, simplifying the visa process and attracting more foreign tourists.

3. **Swadesh Darshan and PRASAD Schemes:** The Swadesh Darshan and PRASAD (Pilgrimage Rejuvenation and Spiritual Augmentation Drive) schemes were implemented to develop and promote tourism in regions with historical, religious or cultural significance.

4. **Infrastructure Development:** Investments have been made to improve tourist infrastructure including airports, roads and connectivity to popular tourist destinations—making travel more convenient and accessible.

5. **Tourist Circuits:** The government identified and developed tourist circuits that link multiple destinations, encouraging tourists to explore diverse regions based on specific themes or cultural contexts.

6. **Sustainable Tourism Initiatives:** There is a focus on promoting sustainable tourism practices to protect the environment and preserve India's natural and cultural heritage for future generations.

7. **Tourism Promotion Events:** India actively participates in international travel fairs and conducts road shows in various countries to attract foreign tourists and showcase its tourism potential.

8. **Regional Connectivity Scheme (UDAN):** The Udan Yojana is a significant initiative introduced by the Indian government to enhance air connectivity to remote regions in the country. Its primary goal is to offer affordable and accessible air travel options to people residing in areas that were previously underserved by aviation services. By facilitating improved connectivity, the scheme contributes to economic growth and development in these regions.

9. **Digital Initiatives:** The government leverages digital platforms and social media to effectively promote tourism and engage with potential travellers.

10. **Branding Initiatives:** India undertakes branding initiatives for specific states and regions, promoting their unique attractions and encouraging tourism beyond popular destinations.

These initiatives demonstrate India's commitment to utilizing tourism as a key driver for economic growth, employment generation and cultural exchange—contributing to the overall development of the nation. By showcasing its rich cultural heritage and investing in tourist infrastructure, India aims to attract both domestic and international tourists and capitalize on the economic opportunities that the tourism industry offers.

The present state of promoting tourism in India has seen positive outcomes with an increase in tourist arrivals, both domestic and international. However, several challenges need to be addressed to further boost the tourism sector:

1. **Infrastructure Development:** While improvements have been made, certain remote and less explored areas lack proper connectivity and tourist facilities, hindering their potential as tourist destinations.

2. **Environmental Concerns:** The influx of tourists can strain natural resources and lead to environmental degradation in popular destinations. Implementing sustainable tourism practices is crucial to protect the environment.

3. **Safety and Security:** Ensuring the safety and security of tourists, especially female travellers, is essential to maintain India's image as a safe and welcoming destination.

4. **Quality of Services:** Maintaining high-quality services—including accommodation, transportation and hygiene—is vital for enhancing the overall tourist experience and promoting repeat visits.

5. **Regulatory Challenges:** Complex regulations and bureaucratic hurdles can discourage investment in the tourism sector and hinder its growth.

6. **Seasonal Imbalance:** Certain destinations experience a surge in tourist arrivals during peak seasons but remain underutilized during the rest of the year, leading to seasonal imbalances.

Measures to overcome the challenges before promoting tourism

To overcome these challenges, India can take several measures:

1. **Infrastructure Development:** Continue investing in infrastructure development, especially in lesser-explored regions, to improve connectivity and facilities.

2. **Sustainable Tourism Practices:** Implement eco-friendly and sustainable tourism practices to preserve the environment and promote responsible tourism.

3. **Safety Measures:** Enhance safety and security measures for tourists through better policing, surveillance and awareness campaigns.

4. **Skill Development:** Provide training and skill-development programs for the tourism workforce to ensure high-quality services and hospitality.

5. **Streamlining Regulations:** Simplify bureaucratic procedures and regulatory processes to attract more investments and facilitate tourism-related businesses.

6. **Promoting Offbeat Destinations:** Focus on promoting lesser-known destinations to distribute tourist footfall more evenly throughout the year and reduce pressure on popular sites.

7. **Digital Marketing:** Leverage digital platforms and social media to effectively market India's tourism potential to a global audience.

8. **Public–Private Partnerships (PPP):** Encourage PPP models to develop and manage tourist facilities, leveraging private-sector expertise.

9. **Specialized Tourist Circuits:** Develop specialized tourist circuits catering to specific interests like adventure tourism, wellness tourism and cultural tourism.

10. **Collaboration with States:** Work closely with state governments to create tourism-friendly policies and support destination-specific initiatives.

By addressing these challenges and implementing strategic measures, India can further enhance its position as a preferred tourist destination—contributing to economic growth, job creation and overall national development.

10 Strategies by which India can promote Tourism

To promote tourism and become a developed nation by 2050, India can undertake the following 10 strategies:

1. **Infrastructure Development:** Invest in improving transportation networks, airports, roads and other essential infrastructure to facilitate easier access to tourist destinations.

2. **Diversification of Tourist Attractions:** Develop and promote a wide range of tourist attractions including cultural heritage sites, natural landscapes, adventure activities and unique experiences to cater to diverse interests.

3. **Sustainable Tourism Practices:** Implement eco-friendly and sustainable tourism practices to preserve the environment and promote responsible tourism.

4. **Marketing and Promotion:** Launch effective global-marketing campaigns to showcase India's tourism potential and attract international travellers.

5. **Skill Development:** Provide training and skill-development programs for the tourism workforce to ensure high-quality services and hospitality.

6. **Safety and Security:** Enhance safety measures for tourists through better policing, surveillance and awareness campaigns to create a safe and welcoming environment.

7. **Digitalization and Innovation:** Utilize digital platforms and innovative technologies to enhance the overall tourist experience such as virtual tours, online bookings and mobile apps.

8. **Public–Private Partnerships (PPP):** Foster collaborations between the government and private sector to develop and manage tourist facilities and attractions, leveraging private-sector expertise.

9. **Specialized Tourist Circuits:** Develop specialized tourist circuits catering to specific interests like adventure tourism, wellness tourism, religious tourism, etc.

10. **Regional and State Collaboration:** Work closely with state governments and local communities to create tourism-friendly policies and support destination-specific initiatives.

Conclusion

Promoting tourism is crucial for India's progress towards becoming a developed nation by 2050. It will lead to economic growth, create jobs, preserve cultural heritage and foster cross-cultural understanding. Investment in infrastructure, sustainable practices and technological advancements will enhance the overall tourist experience. By empowering local communities and showcasing India's diverse attractions, the country will attract more visitors—enhancing its global image and contributing to its development as a developed nation.

Encourage Sports and Fitness

Introduction

Encouraging sports and fitness is vital for India's development as a developed nation. It offers various advantages including improved health, national unity, economic growth, life-skills development, global recognition and social empowerment. By nurturing sporting talent and investing in sports infrastructure, India can excel on the global stage and promote inclusivity. This holistic approach significantly contributes to India's overall progress and development.

Defining Sports and the Benefits of Fitness

Sports and fitness involve activities that promote physical exercise and well-being. Encouraging sports and fitness is crucial for India's development as a developed nation due to its numerous benefits:

1. **Improved Health:** Regular exercise and sports participation lead to better physical and mental health, reducing the risk of chronic diseases and enhancing overall well-being.

2. **National Unity:** Sports events unite people from diverse backgrounds, fostering a sense of national pride and identity.

3. **Economic Growth:** Investment in sports infrastructure and events attracts tourists, generates revenue and creates employment opportunities—contributing to economic growth.

4. **Life-Skills Development:** Sports instil valuable life-skills like discipline, teamwork, leadership and perseverance—enhancing personal growth.

5. **Global Recognition:** Sporting achievements enhance a country's reputation on the global stage, attracting attention and respect from the international community.

6. **Social Empowerment:** Sports empower marginalized communities by providing opportunities for talent showcase and breaking societal barriers.

7. **Nurturing Sporting Talent:** Investing in athlete development produces world-class athletes who bring glory to the nation.

8. **Inclusivity and Diversity:** Sports promote inclusivity, allowing people from diverse backgrounds to participate on equal footing.

9. **Youth Development:** Engaging youth in sports reduces negative involvement and promotes a healthier lifestyle.

10. **Long-term Impact:** Encouraging sports leads to a healthier and more productive workforce, contributing to a stronger nation.

By adopting a holistic approach, India can foster a sporting culture and nurture talent through collaboration between the government, private sector and sports associations. This will lead to overall development, improved citizen well-being and global sporting recognition.

The Present State of Sports and Fitness in India and the Challenges before it

The Indian government, under the leadership of the present administration, has undertaken several initiatives to encourage sports and fitness in the country. Some of the notable efforts include:

1. **Khelo India Program:** The Khelo India initiative was launched in 2018 to promote sports at the grassroots level and identify and nurture young sporting talent. The program provides

financial assistance to athletes; supports sports academies and organizes national and state-level competitions.

2. **Fit-India Movement:** Launched in 2019, the Fit-India Movement is a national campaign that aims to encourage people to adopt a healthy and active lifestyle. It includes various campaigns, events and fitness challenges to raise awareness about the importance of regular exercise and physical fitness.

3. **Sports Infrastructure Development:** The government has been investing in the development of sports infrastructure across the country. This includes the construction of new sports stadiums, training centres and facilities to support various sports disciplines and provide better training opportunities for athletes.

4. **Support to National Sports Federations (NSFs):** The government provides financial assistance and technical support to National Sports Federations and other sports bodies to promote and develop sports in India. This support helps in enhancing the development of sports and supporting athletes.

5. **Hosting International Sporting Events:** India has actively bid for and hosted various international sporting events to promote sports and tourism in the country. Events like the Indian Premier League (IPL), FIFA U-17 World Cup and the Commonwealth Games have been hosted in India in recent years.

6. **Promoting Sports for Women:** Special emphasis has been placed on promoting sports and fitness among women. Various schemes and programs have been implemented to encourage female participation in sports and create opportunities for their growth and development.

7. **Sports Science and Research:** The government has also invested in sports science and research to enhance athlete performance and support talent identification and development.

These initiatives reflect the government's commitment to promoting sports and fitness in India, thus and encouraging a healthier and more active population.

Challenges

India faces several challenges in promoting sports and fitness:

1. **Lack of Professional Coaching:** A shortage of qualified coaches impedes proper talent development.

2. **Sports Governance and Administration:** Inefficiency, corruption and lack of transparency hinder sports growth.

3. **Limited Sports Science and Research:** The absence of advanced training techniques and analysis tools affects athlete development.

4. **Gender Disparity:** Cultural barriers limit the participation of women in sports, perpetuating gender inequality.

5. **Competition from Other Entertainment:** Diverse entertainment options divert attention from sports.

6. **Sports Injuries and Health Concerns:** Risks of injuries and health issues discourage involvement in sports.

7. **Lack of Sports Promotion and Awareness:** Insufficient campaigns limit interest in physical activities.

8. **Long-Term Athlete Development:** The absence of structured programs may hinder India's success in international sports.

Measures to overcome these Challenges

To promote sports and fitness in India and overcome the challenges, a collaborative approach involving the government, sports associations, the private sector, educational institutions and the community is essential. Measures such as awareness campaigns, public–private partnerships, incentives for athletes, promotion of school sports and long-term planning can be implemented. Creating an inclusive environment and continuous assessment of sports policies will contribute to India's sports development, leading to a healthier and more developed nation. By adopting these measures, India can harness its sporting potential and establish itself as a prominent player in the global sports arena.

10 Strategies by which India can encourage Sports and Fitness

Encouraging sports and fitness in India requires a comprehensive and multi-faceted approach. The ten steps that India can undertake to ensure the promotion of sports and fitness are as follows:

1. **Integrate Sports in Education:** Introduce sports as a mandatory part of the school curriculum and provide ample opportunities for students to participate in physical activities.

2. **Grassroots Development:** Establish programs that focus on talent identification and nurture young athletes from the grassroots level. Organize sports competitions and training camps at the district and state levels.

3. **Public–Private Partnerships:** Foster collaborations between the government, the private sector and non-profit organizations to invest in sports infrastructure, coaching and talent-development programs.

4. **Incentives and Scholarships:** Provide incentives such as cash rewards and scholarships to athletes who excel in their respective sports. This will motivate athletes and their families to take sports seriously.

5. **Promoting the Participation of Women:** Support and promote the participation of women in sports by creating gender-specific sports programs, scholarships and facilities. Encourage gender equality in sports and address cultural barriers.

6. **Sports Science and Research:** Invest in sports science and research to enhance athlete performance and prevent injuries.

Establish sports research institutes and sports medicine centres to support athletes' well-being.

7. **Developing Sports Infrastructure:** Develop and upgrade sports infrastructure at the grassroots level, schools, colleges and rural areas. This includes building stadiums, training centres and multipurpose sports facilities.

8. **Professional Sports Leagues:** Encourage the establishment of professional sports leagues in various disciplines. These leagues can provide a platform for athletes to showcase their talents and attract more viewers and sponsors.

9. **Awareness Campaigns:** Launch nationwide awareness campaigns to promote the benefits of sports and fitness. Utilize media platforms, social media and celebrities to reach a broader audience.

10. **Hosting International Sporting Events:** Host international sporting events to showcase India's capabilities and attract global attention. Events like the Olympics, Asian Games or World Championships can boost the country's image and inspire young athletes.

By undertaking these steps, India can create an environment conducive to the growth of sports and fitness—leading to a healthier and more active population, improved performance in international sports events and an enhanced overall quality of life for its citizens. Encouraging sports and fitness will not only contribute to the physical well-being of the population but also boost the country's overall development and soft power on the global stage.

Conclusion

Encouraging sports and fitness is a critical factor in India's journey towards becoming a developed country by 2050. By promoting sports at all levels, investing in infrastructure, supporting athletes and fostering a culture of fitness, India can achieve numerous benefits. These include improved physical health, economic growth, social cohesion and global recognition. Integrating sports education, public–private partnerships and hosting international events will further enhance sports development. The impact extends beyond health, as a successful sports industry can create economic opportunities and global prestige. Embracing sports and fitness will not only contribute to India's development but also inspire future generations to excel in sports, positioning India as a developed nation by 2050.

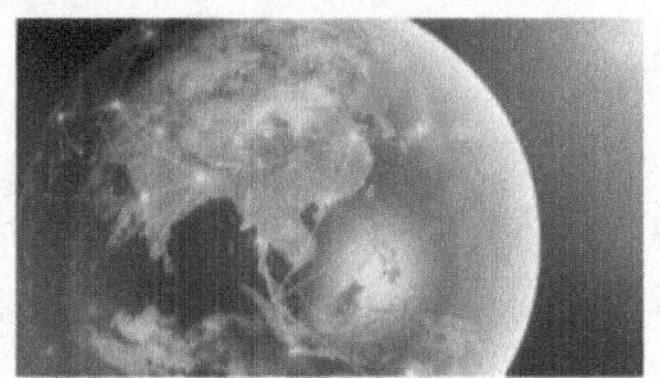

Foster International Collaboration

Introduction

Fostering international collaboration is crucial for India's development in the 21st century. In an increasingly interconnected world, collaboration allows for joint efforts to tackle global challenges such as climate change and terrorism. By engaging with other nations, India gains access to valuable resources, technology and expertise—which can promote economic growth and facilitate international trade. Knowledge and skill transfer through collaboration contribute to the development of India's human capital.

Scientific cooperation drives advancements and innovation, while cultural exchange fosters global harmony and mutual understanding. Moreover, collaborative efforts play a pivotal role in ensuring peace and security, strengthening diplomatic relations and addressing health challenges and sustainable development. By actively fostering international collaboration, India positions itself as a responsible global player, accelerating its journey towards becoming a developed nation by 2050.

Defining International Collaboration

International collaboration is when countries and organizations work together to address common challenges, share knowledge and pursue shared goals. For India's development as a developed nation by 2050, fostering international collaboration is crucial. It provides access to resources, technology and expertise—accelerating growth across sectors and opening new markets for Indian products. Collaborating also enables effective collective action on global challenges like climate change and terrorism.

Through international collaboration, India benefits from knowledge transfer, scientific advancements and human capital development. Cultural exchange enhances global harmony and strengthened diplomatic relations bolsters India's standing in the international community. Collaborative efforts contribute to regional and global peace, address health challenges and promote sustainable development goals.

By actively fostering international collaboration, India can leverage collective wisdom and opportunities—positioning itself as a responsible global player and making significant progress towards becoming a developed nation by 2050.

The Present State of international collaboration as exercised by India has several challenges before it; measures need to be taken to overcome them. India has actively pursued international collaboration through bilateral and multilateral partnerships, economic initiatives, participation in regional and global forums, trade agreements, defence collaborations, space cooperation, climate-change efforts, health and research collaborations, educational and cultural exchanges and the COVID-19 pandemic response. These efforts aim to enhance economic ties, technology collaborations, defence capabilities, space missions, climate-change mitigation, healthcare, education and global cooperation. (It is essential to acknowledge that international relations are dynamic and may have evolved to a great extent)

India has made significant progress in fostering international collaboration across various sectors. However, some challenges need to be addressed to further strengthen and leverage these collaborations to achieve the goal of becoming a developed country.

The Present State of International Collaboration and the Challenges before it

India has made significant progress in fostering international collaboration across various sectors, as evident from the following areas:

1. **Economic Cooperation:** India has developed strong economic ties with numerous countries and actively participates in international trade and investment. The country has become an attractive destination for foreign direct investment (FDI) and has engaged in numerous bilateral and multilateral trade agreements, promoting economic growth and global integration.

2. **Defence and Security Partnerships:** India has actively pursued defence collaborations with several nations, participating in joint military exercises and signing technology transfer agreements. These collaborations aim to enhance India's defence capabilities and promote regional security and stability.

3. **Space Exploration and Research:** India has successfully collaborated with international space agencies on various space missions and satellite launches. The country's space agency, the Indian Space Research Organization (ISRO), has demonstrated its expertise in space technology through these collaborations.

4. **Climate Change and Renewable-Energy Initiatives:** India is actively involved in global efforts to combat climate change and reduce greenhouse gas emissions. The country has made commitments to increase its renewable-energy capacity and is actively participating in international climate-change negotiations and initiatives.

5. **Healthcare and Pharma Collaboration:** India is a major player in the global pharmaceutical industry and has collaborated with international organizations for healthcare initiatives and research. The country's pharmaceutical sector has been instrumental in supplying affordable medicines to various regions across the world.

Fostering international collaboration presents various challenges for India, which need to be fully addressed to ensure effective and fruitful partnerships. These challenges include geopolitical complexities and diplomatic relations that may hinder seamless cooperation with certain countries. Furthermore, there is a need for robust infrastructure and effective institutions to facilitate successful collaborations. India must invest in research and development to attract high-tech collaborations and stay competitive globally. Harmonizing regulatory and policy frameworks is crucial for creating a conducive environment for international partnerships. Bridging cultural and linguistic barriers through language training and cultural exchanges is vital for effective communication with diverse partners. Overcoming these challenges will allow India to leverage the benefits of global cooperation and accelerate its development as a developed nation by 2050.

To overcome the challenges in fostering international collaboration, India can implement the following measures:

1. **Strengthen Diplomatic Ties:** Continue efforts to enhance diplomatic relations with other countries through dialogues, resolving disputes and building trust and mutual understanding—creating a conducive environment for collaborations.

2. **Invest in Infrastructure and R&D:** Focus on building world-class infrastructure and invest in research and development to attract foreign partners and enable smoother collaborations in cutting-edge technologies.

3. **Simplify Regulatory Processes:** Streamline regulatory and policy frameworks to make it easier for foreign entities to invest and collaborate in India, reducing bureaucratic hurdles.

4. **Promote Education and Skill Development:** Emphasize education and skill development to produce a competent and skilled workforce capable of participating in international projects and fostering knowledge transfer.

5. **Promote Public–Private Partnerships:** Encourage public–private partnerships to leverage the strengths of both sectors and undertake large-scale collaborative projects that benefit the nation and the international community.

6. **Encourage Cultural Exchanges:** Promote cultural exchanges and language learning to foster better understanding and communication between Indian and foreign partners, enhancing cooperation and synergy.

7. **Focus on Sustainability:** Incorporate sustainability and environmentally friendly practices in collaborations to align with global goals and attract partners with similar objectives, demonstrating India's commitment to sustainable development.

8. **Active Participation in International Forums:** Engage actively in regional and global forums to voice India's concerns, seek support and foster greater cooperation with international partners.

9. **Enhance Digital Connectivity:** Improve digital connectivity to facilitate seamless communication and data sharing between collaborators, promoting efficient exchange of information and ideas.

10. **Establish Clear Objectives:** Clearly define the objectives and mutual benefits of collaborations to ensure that all parties are committed to the partnership's success to achieve the desired outcomes.

By implementing these measures, India can effectively overcome the challenges and create an environment conducive to international collaboration, harnessing the benefits of global cooperation to accelerate its journey towards becoming a developed nation by 2050.

India can thus foster stronger international collaboration—leading to mutual growth and progress—and ultimately contribute to its development as a developed country by 2050.

The 10 Steps that India can undertake to foster international collaboration

1. **Strengthen Diplomatic Ties:** India should prioritize the enhancement of diplomatic relations with other nations through regular high-level engagements, bilateral meetings and diplomatic summits. Building strong political connections is crucial for fostering collaboration.

2. **Invest in Infrastructure and R&D:** Continued investment in world-class infrastructure and research and development will attract foreign partners and facilitate collaborative projects in various sectors.

3. **Simplify Regulatory Processes:** Streamlining regulatory and policy frameworks will make it easier for foreign businesses and investors to navigate India's market and foster partnerships.

4. **Promote Education and Skill Development:** Emphasize education and skill development to produce a competent and skilled workforce capable of engaging in international projects and collaborations.

5. **Promote Public–Private Partnerships:** Encourage public–private partnerships to leverage the strengths of both sectors and undertake large-scale collaborative initiatives.

6. **Actively Participate in International Forums:** India should actively engage in regional and global forums to represent its

interests, seek support and foster greater cooperation with other countries.

7. **Focus on Sustainability:** Incorporate sustainability and environmentally friendly practices in collaborations to align with global goals and attract partners with similar objectives.

8. **Facilitate Cultural Exchanges:** Promote cultural exchanges and language learning to foster better understanding and communication between Indian and foreign partners.

9. **Encourage Digital Connectivity:** Improve digital connectivity to facilitate seamless communication and data sharing between collaborators from different parts of the world.

10. **Establish Clear Objectives:** Clearly define the objectives and mutual benefits of collaborations to ensure all parties are committed to the partnership's success and long-term goals.

By implementing these steps, India can create a favourable environment for international collaboration, attract foreign investments, access advanced technologies and share knowledge and expertise. This will enable India to leverage the strengths of global partnerships to accelerate its economic growth, social development and overall progress towards becoming a developed country by 2050.

Conclusion

Fostering international collaboration is crucial for India's development, as it provides access to advanced technologies, foreign direct investment and knowledge sharing—accelerating industrial growth and improving the competitiveness of the workforce. It opens up new market access and export opportunities, leading to economic prosperity and infrastructure development. Collaborating with other nations also enables India to address global challenges, promote cultural exchange and strengthen diplomatic ties. By engaging in research and innovation, India can become a knowledge-based economy and actively participate in shaping global policies. Overall, fostering international collaboration is essential for India's development journey, allowing the country to leverage global partnerships and achieve its vision of becoming a developed nation by 2050.

India at the Centre Stage of the World - Realizing the Vision for 2050

Introduction

India, with its ancient wisdom and the world's oldest civilization, envisions a future where it stands at the centre stage of the world by 2050. As the largest democracy and one of the most populous nations, India holds immense potential to play a key role in establishing a global democracy that fosters the betterment of the world. This article explores the two foundational pillars of India's vision for global leadership: promoting global citizenship education and fostering international cooperation. By realizing these 21 visions, India aims to shape a brighter and more interconnected future for the world.

Pillar 1: Global Citizenship Education - Empowering Responsible Global Citizens

Global Citizenship Education is a critical aspect of India's vision for the future. It seeks to equip individuals, especially the youth, with the knowledge, skills, attitudes and values necessary to engage effectively with global issues. By nurturing a sense of responsibility towards addressing pressing global challenges, India aims to create responsible and proactive global citizens. The following are the transformative impacts of Global Citizenship Education:

1. **Cultivating Responsible Global Citizens:** Empowering Indian youth with knowledge, skills and values to engage responsibly

with global issues fosters a sense of global citizenship. These responsible global citizens will contribute to international cooperation, collaborative problem-solving and efforts to address global challenges.

2. **Global Leadership and Innovation:** Nurturing entrepreneurship and promoting innovation among Indian youth can lead to ground-breaking solutions for global issues. India's innovative prowess can contribute to advancements in science, technology and sustainable development—establishing it as a leader in shaping the global agenda.

3. **Cross-Cultural Understanding and Cooperation:** By promoting sports, arts and cultural exchange programs, India can bridge cultural divides and promote understanding among nations. Building strong cultural ties enhances diplomatic relations and fosters peaceful international interactions.

4. **Advocacy for Global Causes:** Equipped with digital literacy and critical thinking skills, Indian youth can advocate for global causes through online activism and advocacy. They can amplify the voices of marginalized communities, champion human rights and contribute to global movements for justice and equality.

5. **Strengthening Global Diplomacy:** Nurturing future leaders who value empathy and understanding enables India to play a key role in international diplomacy. Empathetic leaders are more likely to engage in constructive dialogues, build trust and seek peaceful resolutions to conflicts—promoting global stability.

Pillar 2: Fostering International Cooperation - Embracing a Global Collaborative Approach

Alongside Global Citizenship Education, fostering international cooperation is fundamental to India's vision for global leadership in 2050. By collaborating with other nations, India aims to address complex global challenges, seize growth opportunities and contribute to the progress of the world. The key elements of India's approach to fostering international cooperation include:

1. **Strengthening Economic Ties and Strategic Partnerships:** India seeks to enhance its global economic standing by promoting trade, attracting foreign direct investment and facilitating technology transfer through strategic partnerships with other nations.

2. **Embracing Emerging Technologies and Innovation:** By becoming a leader in sectors like information technology, artificial intelligence, renewable energy and space exploration, India can drive global advancements and contribute to solutions for shared challenges.

3. **Prioritizing Sustainable Development:** India aims to address environmental challenges and promote sustainable practices, including transitioning to clean-energy sources and advocating for eco-friendly policies at the global level.

4. **Utilizing Soft-Power Assets:** India's cultural heritage, traditions and soft-power assets—such as Bollywood, yoga and Ayurveda—can enhance its global influence and strengthen diplomatic relationships with other countries.

5. **Active Participation in International Organizations:** India seeks to actively engage in international organizations and initiatives to contribute to policy discussions on critical issues like climate change, public health and more.

6. **Providing Humanitarian Aid and Development Assistance:** As a responsible global player, India prioritizes providing humanitarian aid and development assistance to nations facing crises or challenges, demonstrating its commitment to global well-being.

7. **Investing in Education and Skill Development:** India recognizes the significance of equipping its youth with the knowledge and abilities to lead on the global stage, making education and skill development a priority.

Becoming a Leader of Global Democracy

To establish itself as a leader of global democracy, India must demonstrate a commitment to democratic values, human rights and inclusive governance. Combining efforts in fostering international cooperation and promoting global citizenship education, India can take crucial steps towards this vision:

1. **Democratic Values:** India can advocate for democratic values, freedom of speech, rule of law and respect for human rights on the international stage, setting an example for other nations to follow.

2. **Inclusive Governance:** By promoting inclusive governance practices at home and supporting inclusive initiatives abroad, India exemplifies the importance of diverse voices in decision-making processes.

3. **Humanitarian Aid and Development Assistance:** As a global democracy leader, India can prioritize providing humanitarian aid and development assistance to countries facing crises or challenges.

4. **Responsible Global Diplomacy:** India's influence can be used to support democratic reforms, fair elections and the protection of democratic institutions under threat, all of which actively contribute to global democracy.

5. **Soft-Power Projection:** By emphasizing cultural exchanges and promoting Indian culture globally, India can project a positive image and strengthen diplomatic ties with other nations.

6. **Digital Connectivity:** Emphasizing digital literacy and responsible media consumption among its citizens can enable India to engage in informed and constructive discussions on global issues.

7. **Support for Democratic Institutions:** By providing support and technical assistance to strengthen democratic institutions in other countries, India actively contributes to the development and sustenance of robust democratic systems globally.

8. **Improvement of international institutions:** India is well positioned to advocate for a reform of international institutions such as the United Nations to make them deliver better in the best interest of the world's citizens, including those in India. This involves strengthening the UN's democratic and representative character, for instance through the creation of a World Parliamentary Assembly.

Conclusion

India's vision for global leadership by 2050 is firmly grounded in the principles of promoting global citizenship education and fostering international cooperation. Through these pillars, India aims to create responsible, empathetic and proactive citizens who understand their role in shaping a better world and are prepared to contribute to societal and global progress. By demonstrating a commitment to democratic values and embracing international collaboration, India can indeed stand at the centre stage of the world—leading by example and contributing positively to a more peaceful, inclusive and prosperous global community.

References

1. Boin, Arjen. "The Anthem Companion to Philip Selznick. VanSeters, Paul, Anthem Press. 2021. 234 Pp." Public Administration, August 29, 2022. https://doi.org/10.1111/padm.12886.

2. Briefing, India. "India's G20 Presidency and Asian Trade Implications - India Briefing News." India Briefing News, February 2, 2023. https://www.india-briefing.com/news/indias-g20-presidency-and-asian-trade-implications-27090.html/.

3. Cai, Penghong. "The Changing Regional Architectures in Asia and Their Potential Implications." China Quarterly of International Strategic Studies 01, no. 04 (December 2015): 591–607. https://doi.org/10.1142/s2377740015500281.

4. Carlson, Brian G. "Andrea Kendall-Taylor/David Shullman: Navigating the Deepening Russia-China Partnership. Washington, DC: Center for a New American Security, Januar 2021." SIRIUS – Zeitschrift Für Strategische Analysen 5, no. 3 (August 1, 2021): 291–92. https://doi.org/10.1515/sirius-2021-3009.

5. Chaudhury, Dipanjan Roy. "India at the Helm: Future Directions for the SCO." RIAC :: India at the Helm: Future Directions for the SCO, March 10, 2023. https://russiancouncil.ru/en/analytics-and-comments/columns/asian-kaleidoscope/india-at-the-helm-future-directions-for-the-sco/.

6. Economy of India - Wikipedia. "Economy of India - Wikipedia," June 1, 2022. https://en.wikipedia.org/wiki/Economy_of_India#:~:text=The%20economy%20of%20India%20has,purchasing%20power%20parity%20(PPP).

7. Harvard Business Review. "The U.S.–India Relationship Is Key to the Future of Tech," April 17, 2023. https://hbr.org/2023/04/the-u-s-india-relationship-is-key-to-the-future-of-tech.

8. Hindustan Times. "How India Can Benefit from SCO," November 25, 2020. https://www.hindustantimes.com/analysis/how-india-can-benefit-from-sco/story-lvHNVzB99Asw6EPcgfE6NK.html.

9. House, The White. "Joint Statement of the Leaders of India, Israel, United Arab Emirates, and the United States (I2U2) | The White House." The White House, July 14, 2022. https://www.whitehouse.gov/briefing-room/statements-releases/2022/07/14/joint-statement-of-the-leaders-of-india-israel-united-arab-emirates-and-the-united-states-i2u2/.

10. Jörgensen, Kirsten, and Christian Wagner. "Low Carbon Governance in Multi-Level Structures: EU-India Relations on Energy and Climate." Environmental Policy and Governance 27, no. 2 (March 2017): 137–48. https://doi.org/10.1002/eet.1749.

11. List of countries by GDP growth 1980–2010 - Wikipedia. "List of Countries by GDP Growth 1980–2010 - Wikipedia," October 24, 2020. https://en.wikipedia.org/wiki/List_of_countries_by_GDP_growth_1980%E2%80%932010.

12. Mansfield, Edward D. "Rising Powers in the Global Economy: Issues and Questions." International Studies Review 16, no. 3 (September 2014): 437–42. https://doi.org/10.1111/misr.12148.

13. Sahgal, Ram. "India to Add a Trillion Dollars to GDP Every 12-18 Months within a Decade: Adani." mint, November 19, 2022. https://www.livemint.com/news/india/india-to-add-a-trillion-dollars-to-gdp-every-12-18-months-within-a-decade-adani-11668851732612.html.

14. Salter, Brian. "State Strategies and the Geopolitics of the Global Knowledge Economy: China, India and the Case of Regenerative Medicine." Geopolitics 14, no. 1 (February 13, 2009): 47–78. https://doi.org/10.1080/14650040802578666.

15. Standard, Business, and @bsindia. "India Adds 23 Unicorns in 2022, Overtakes China for 2nd Consecutive Year." India adds 23 unicorns in 2022, overtakes China for 2nd consecutive year, March 15, 2023. https://www.business-standard.com/article/companies/india-adds-23-unicorns-in-2022-overtakes-china-for-2nd-consecutive-year-123031500825_1.html.

16. SULTAN, Beenish. "China' s Role in BRICS & Relevance to GCC-China Relations: Complementarities & Conflicting Interests." Journal of Middle Eastern and Islamic Studies (in Asia) 10, no. 2 (June 2016): 71–98. https://doi.org/10.1080/19370679.2016.12023283.

17. The Economic Times. "India's Economic Resilience: IMF Predicts Indian Economy Will Grow by Nearly 6 per Cent This Fiscal Year," n.d. https://economictimes.indiatimes.com/news/economy/indicators/indias-economic-resilience-imf-predicts-indian-economy-will-grow-by-nearly-6-per-cent-this-fiscal-year/articleshow/99842943.cms.

18. Trade. "EU Trade Relations with India," February 6, 2023. https://policy.trade.ec.europa.eu/eu-trade-relationships-country-and-region/countries-and-regions/india_en.

19. Wen Zhou. "Comparing the Economic Growth of China and India: Current Situation, Problems, and Prospects." World

Review of Political Economy 5, no. 4 (December 1, 2014). https://doi.org/10.13169/worlrevipoliecon.5.4.0455.

20. What Does India Gain From the Shanghai Cooperation Organization? – The Diplomat. "What Does India Gain From the Shanghai Cooperation Organization?," May 1, 2023. https://thediplomat.com/2023/05/what-does-india-gain-from-the-shanghai-cooperation-organization/.

21. www.ETEnergyworld.com. "India to Be 2nd Largest Economy by 2050, to Add a Trillion Dollar to GDP Every 12-18 Months: Adani - ET EnergyWorld." ETEnergyworld.com, n.d. https://energy.economictimes.indiatimes.com/news/renewable/india-to-be-2nd-largest-economy-by-2050-to-add-a-trillion-dollar-to-gdp-every-12-18-months-adani/95632254.

22. Lectures by Professor Alexandre Lambert at GSD

23. Rossow, Richard M. "The United States' 2023 Agenda for Building a Stronger Relationship with India." The United States' 2023 Agenda for Building a Stronger Relationship with India, n.d. https://www.csis.org/analysis/united-states-2023-agenda-building-stronger-relationship-india."What

24. Watch for in 2023." C&EN Global Enterprise 100, no. 44 (December 19, 2022): 38–39. https://doi.org/10.1021/cen-10044-cover8.

About the Author

 **Dr. Shishir Srivastava** is a notable figure in the field of international relations, career counselling and motivational speaking. With over 23 years of experience, he has gained recognition for his expertise in guiding students, young adults and parents. He holds a certification in Organizational Leadership from the Harvard Business School, and he completed a four-month diploma course in international relations at the Geneva School of Diplomacy focusing on Geopolitics, Global Environment Policies and International Law. He has a master's degree in counselling psychology and a Post-Graduate Diploma in Human Rights Management (PGDHRM).

Dr. Srivastava has made significant contributions to education, counselling and building international relations since January 1st, 2000, when he started serving his alma mater, City Montessori School (CMS) in Lucknow, India, which is the world's largest school in a single city with over 61,000 students. At CMS, he served as the Head of the Personality Development and Career Counselling Department from 2005 to 2016; and since 2017, he holds the position of Head of the International Relations Department. Since 2001, he has been playing a significant role in the organizational aspects of the International Conferences of Chief Justices of the World. For the past 23 years, these annual conferences have seen participation of 1429 chief justices and judges from 139 countries.

CMS founders, Dr. Jagdish Gandhi & Dr. Bharti Gandhi, along with CMS MD & President, Prof. Geeta Gandhi Kingdon, have been inspirational figures in the life of Dr. Srivastava.

As an international motivational speaker, Dr. Shishir Srivastava has conducted workshops and training sessions in various countries, including Switzerland, Russia, Japan, Spain, Norway and Malaysia. His extensive travels, covering 22 countries, have allowed him to empower and guide individuals through his motivational speeches.

Dr. Srivastava is also a published author, and this is his fourth book. One of his notable works is the bestselling book titled 'The Eight Powers Within You' (Penguin Books, 2010). His book 'Utho Yuva' (Youth Arise!) has also garnered appreciation, including praise from the Prime Minister, Shri. Narendra Modi. He has been awarded titles such as 'Global Friend of World's Children' (Sweden, 2006) and 'Man of the Year' (Chennai, 2011). In 2021, in recognition of his long-standing contributions to the field of education, he was awarded an Honorary Doctorate in Education by Theophany University, Haiti.

Outside of his professional life, Dr. Shishir Srivastava finds solace in reading the Bhagwad Gita during his leisure time. He and his wife, Sophia, have a 21-year-old son, Srijan, who is a music composer based in Germany. For more details, please check: www.drshishir.in